What's wrong
With
Christian Rock?

Library of Congress Catalog Card No: 90-085347

ISBN: 0-937958-36-0

First Printing

177/A

Published by CHICK PUBLICATIONS
P.O. Box 662 • Chino, CA 91708-0662
Printed in the United States of America

Contents

WHAT'S RIGHT?:

INTERNATIONAL DISTRIBUTORS

Comic-Traktate-Versand
Postfach 3009
5632 Wermelskirchen 3
West Germany

Christ Is The Answer, Inc.
Box 5167, Station A
Toronto, Ont. M5W 1N5, Canada
(416) 699-7800

Chick Publications Distributor
P.O. Box 50096
Porirua, Wellington, New Zealand

Penfold Book & Bible House
P.O. Box 26
Bicester, Oxon, England OX6 8PB
Tel: 0869-249574

Evangelistic Literature Enterprise
P.O. Box 10
Strathpine, Q'ld., Australia 4500
Phone: (07) 205-7100

Is "Christian" Rock Controlled By Satan?

If you've read my first two books, "The Devil's Disciples" and "Dancing With Demons," you know that all secular Rock music is totally under Satan's control. But what about C-Rock ("Christian" Rock)? What about CCM (Contemporary Christian Music)? The devil can't touch those, can he?

Not only can Satan touch them, he OWNS 99% of what passes for Christian music today! Don't believe it? Fasten your seat belt and read this book. CCM covers a wide range of styles, but MOST of it is plain old Rock & Roll.

Whether it's called "Christian" Rock, Heavenly Metal, "Christian" Rap, "Christian" Thrash or Contemporary Christian Music, Rock is still the root, and the devil is the power source behind it.

This book will prove that Satan has his hand in every type of music under the sun. The only music he can't touch is true, scriptural, godly music that brings real praise and honor to God. Everything else belongs to Satan because he is the god of this world and all that is in it (Luke 4:5-8).

Unfortunately, true, godly music doesn't sell 100,000 albums at a crack, and is seldom found on the Top 40 Christian Hit Parade.

There's no nice way to expose sin and rebuke wrongdoing. The only way is to drag it out into the light of God's Word. That's why you'll find this book full of what the Bible says about music, compromise and wickedness. Everything you're about to read was written for one purpose only:

TO WARN ANYONE WHO WILL LISTEN TO STOP PLAYING GAMES WITH GOD BEFORE IT'S TOO LATE!

Did you know CCM is full of occultism, witchcraft, blasphemy and the New Age? In the pages that follow, the biggest names in CCM will convict themselves out of their own mouth. If you want the truth about "Christian" Rock and all that goes with it, the proof is right in your hands.

It's my prayer that through this book the Holy Spirit will pierce your heart with the shocking reality behind one of the greatest deceptions of our modern age:

"Christian" Rock is the music of:

ANTICHRIST!

1

What's Wrong With Christian Rock's Fruit?

In 1985, the Lord Jesus Christ put my wife and me into this ministry to expose Satan's dirty work in popular music. Nearly six years, dozens of meetings and several thousand letters have gone by since then. The Lord Jesus has taught us many things, but one of His greatest lessons is found in the following scripture:

> "Beware of false prophets, which come to you in sheep's clothing, but inwardly they are ravening wolves. Ye shall know them by their fruits... A good tree cannot bring forth evil fruit, neither can a corrupt tree bring forth good fruit. Every tree that bringeth not forth good fruit is hewn down, and cast into the fire. Wherefore by their fruits ye shall know them."   Matthew 7:15,16,18-20

Those verses have a very simple meaning - FALSE PROPHETS ARE KNOWN BY THEIR ROTTEN FRUITS. Most "Christian" Rock defenders believe the "clean" lifestyles and glowing speeches of their C-Rock and CCM idols are C-Rock's fruit.

Not true! The C-Rock and CCM "fruit" is rebellion, and the fans are full of it! The rebellious lives of "Christian" Rock's fans are the real fruit of these modern musical prophets.

Is this fruit godly and good – or wicked and corrupt? The Word of God has much to say about this issue, and anyone who claims Jesus Christ as their personal Saviour should have no problem accepting the Bible as the final authority. With that in mind, let's take a walk through the "Christian" Rock orchard.

In the years we've been involved in this ministry, my wife and I have had the privilege of meeting many hundreds of Christian teens and young adults at our Rock music seminars and other speaking engagements across the country. When the total hypocrisy behind "Christian" Rock is revealed to them, four reactions usually follow:

1.) **ANGER**
2.) **CONFUSION**
3.) **DENIAL**
4.) **DELUSION**

Here's an in-depth examination of each one:

ANGER

When confronted with the truth about C-Rock's ungodliness, the average fan fires back with all guns blazing:

> "What gives YOU the right to judge? What about all the good work these people do, feeding the hungry and helping the poor? They talk about teen suicide and staying pure until marriage. They're anti-dope and pro-God. How DARE you put them down?"

These are all valid points. Let's see how the Bible addresses them.

1.) "What gives YOU the right to judge another person's ministry?"

According to Leviticus 19:15, Matthew 7:1-5, & John 7:24, ANY Christian has the right to match anything against the Bible. If a ministry is truly of God, it will match up perfectly with the Bible. The problem comes when the things in question violate the Word of God. THAT'S when people get mad – when hypocrisy is unmasked and laid bare for all to see.

James 1:20 says, "For the wrath of man worketh not the righteousness of God." If you get MAD when I question your favorite music or star, this

9

is powerful proof of Satan's influence in your life (2 Peter 2:19). Idol worshipers get angry when their idols are pulled down (Judges 6:25-30).

2.) But what about all those "good" works done by "Christian" Rockers?

2 Corinthians 3:1,2 proves the Apostle Paul could care less about letters of recommendation from anyone concerning his good works. The fact that CCM stars throw their weight behind good causes shouldn't overly impress you. There are several reasons why:

The Satan-worshipping secular music stars do the same thing! They're up to their evil necks in Live Aids, Hear N' Aids, Aid For Africa, Farm Aids, Earth Aid and Aid for AIDS. As long as they keep getting free publicity, those chumps will play Aid concerts till the cows come home. Does that make them Christians?

Such activity is any Christian's REASONABLE SERVICE (Romans 12:1-3). Pumped-up brownie points may look good on a Christian resume' and boost record sales, but that doesn't mean God is glorified. Even the BEST of these musicians' good works doesn't impress God (Isaiah 64:6).

CONFUSION

As his anger fades, the average CCM fan falls

into confusion: "But my favorite CCM star wouldn't do that, would they? How can they talk about Jesus, and still be doing the Devil's work? Why would Satan tell people about JESUS? That would be a pretty stupid thing for him to do, wouldn't it?"

Consider the following quote to get your answer:

> "If we continue on this path, respectable, industrious and honest, if we fulfill our duty faithfully, it is my conviction, the Lord God will continually help us in the future. He will not leave respectable people in the lurch indefinitely. He may test them, but in the end He lets His sun shine upon them and gives them His blessing."[1]

Guess who spoke this profound spiritual truth? Billy Graham? Martin Luther, perhaps? Could it have been John Wesley, Jonathan Edwards, or some other great Christian leader from the past? No! The author of those words was:

Adolf Hitler!

Talk is always cheap. It's the FRUIT behind the words that really counts.

Anyone who takes "Christian" Rock at its media-hyped face value has fallen into deep deception. If you believe everything you read and hear about "Christian" Rock, the simple truth is this:

YOU DON'T KNOW YOUR ENEMY! (1 Peter 5:8, 2 Corinthians 2:11). Jesus Christ doesn't need a commercial from the Devil, as Acts 16:16-18 shows so well:

> "And it came to pass, as we went to prayer, a certain damsel possessed of a spirit of divination met us, which brought her masters much gain by soothsaying: The same followed Paul and us, and cried, saying, These men are the servants of the most high God, which shew unto us the way of salvation. And this did she many days. But Paul, being grieved, turned and said to the spirit, I command thee in the name of Jesus Christ to come out of her. And he came out the same hour."

That demon-possessed girl was well able to proclaim God's truth. What does Satan gain from "Christian" Rock? The answer lies in one word - CONFUSION.

> "For where envying and strife is, there is confusion and every evil work." James 3:16

God is not in the business of confusing His people (1 Corinthians 14:33). But Satan is (John 8:44).

Are you confused about "Christian" Rock? The only thing that will bring you out of it is the WHOLE Word of God (John 17:17), combined with the leading of the Holy Ghost (John 16:13). The Bible lays this out perfectly:

12

> "Through thy precepts I get understanding:
> therefore I hate every false way. Thy word
> is a lamp unto my feet, and a light unto my
> path."   Psalm 119:104,105

Confusion always breeds more confusion, and it isn't long until C-Rock followers start making excuses like these:

1.) "Why don't you just let God be God? He'll work it all out in the end. When judgment day comes, we'll know who was right and who was wrong."

People who use this half-baked reasoning are really admitting they simply don't KNOW right from wrong! Here's the good news – you don't have to wait until Judgment Day to find out. The Bible will tell you right now.

This is when C-Rock fans hit the roof and blow their tops. When God's Word exposes this spiritual con game for what it is, those enslaved by it have only two choices. They can get right with God and come out of it – or get really mad and try to justify their sin. When anyone tries to justify evil, confusion is guaranteed to reign supreme.

2.) "I Know my own heart is right, and that's all God cares about. As long as the heart's right, everything else is O.K., right?"

Really? Compare 1 Kings 11:38 and Exodus 15:26

to Deuteronomy 12:8 and Judges 17:6. You'll find that we are to do what God's Word says is right, not what we THINK is right in our own heart. The heart is desperately wicked and deceitful (Jeremiah 17:9,10). "Let your conscience be your guide?" That creed is a lying New Age smoke-screen for the universal rule of all satanism: "Do What Thou Wilt Shall Be The Whole of the Law".

DENIAL

The next step down the deception ladder for an angry, confused CCM addict is denial. Here are some of the most common excuses:

1.) "I pray for protection before I listen to the music or go to the concerts, so everything's O.K."

Would it be OK to smoke some crack cocaine or visit a prostitute, as long as you prayed and asked God's protection first? Of course not. The same goes for participating in Satan's music. If something is of God, you don't have to ask Him to protect you from it. If it's not of God, why mess with it in the first place? Jesus set the record straight when he told Satan:

> "Thou shalt not tempt the Lord thy God."
> Luke 4:12

2.) "I can listen to anything I want, and it doesn't affect me."

That's the problem: It HAS affected you – you just don't know it! It's the spirit of REBELLION making you say those very words.

3.) I was once a sinner, and God is using me. Why can't He do the same with the music?

Converted sinners get new hearts. They are "born-again" (John 3:3). They become "new creatures" (2 Cor. 5:17). They become children of God (1 John 5:13). Rock music always has and always will belong to Satan. God wants nothing to do with the devil's filth.

4.) I'm well-grounded in the Word, so Satan can't deceive me."

1 Corinthians 10:12 proves otherwise:

> "Wherefore let him that thinketh he standeth take heed lest he fall."

DELUSION

One short step away from smug denial lies deep delusion. This next feeble excuse proves the C-Rock stars have trained their flock well to explain away sin:

"I prayed about my music, and the Holy Spirit didn't convict me that it was wrong, so it must be OK."

If that's your excuse, please read Ezekiel 14:1-5. Those verses speak loud and clear. Until we clean the idols out of our life, God will tell us JUST WHAT WE WANT TO HEAR! Is that fair? Of course it is. If you have the audacity to come to God demanding that He approve your sin, why shouldn't He give you what you want?

God doesn't HAVE to convict us to forsake something that clearly violates His Holy Word. True Christians are supposed to know better. Why? Because they read their Bible! If God says it's wrong, it's wrong. (For scriptural proof that C-Rock is not of God, see chapter 17.)

Here's another possibility: Many a C-Rock fan has become so violent in their deluded defense of an ungodly, wicked mockery of Christian music they can't HEAR the Holy Spirit's voice anymore!

A young Christian couple in Australia sent me a letter recently. They are former C-Rockers who have been led out of that delusion by the Holy Spirit and the Word of God. Boldly witnessing the truth about CCM bondage, they are heart-broken at the wall of smug arrogance surrounding them. Their pastor told them to repent on their knees for being "unbalanced." They even witnessed to one of Australia's major Christian outreach centers. Here's how the organization replied:

"Firstly, to answer your letter, the Bible does not say anything directly about rock music – in fact anything it does say about music is positive – so to form a hard and fast doctrine on the subject is not Scripturally sound... Finally any doctrine or belief concerning rock music is entirely opinion, including mine. If you consider Christian rock sinful, it would be wrong for you to listen to it. I play and listen unto God, and draw closer to Him through it. I am not to judge you, nor you me. I will continue with it..."[2]

The Christian who wrote those words should be ashamed. HE'S the one who ought to repent on his knees! He's using the same lame excuse to justify his sin as the SECULAR Rock stars. Read these comments by *KISS* singer Paul Stanley:

"It's always interesting that people tend to interpret the Bible any way that they see fit in terms of how it applies to rock n' roll... Everybody has to decide for themself what works and what doesn't work and what works for me. I'm certainly not in a position where I should be telling people to live their lives the way I live MY life, but likewise neither should you be doing it... I respect you for what you're doing, and it's unfortunate you don't do the same for us. That's too bad..."[3]

Something's dead wrong when Christians use the same ungodly excuses as the perverts in *KISS* to justify their wickedness!

This quote by a Christian bookstore owner in Texas shows why so many Christian youth are completely deluded about the music they listen to. He's describing a new type of "Christian" Punk called "Thrash":

> "I regard this music, the lyrics, the dress, the performance, and lifestyle of the artists to be in a grey area which we will currently accept, but hopefully be constantly sensitive to the Spirit, whom we trust will keep us from even the slightest compromise, from that which is His highest will, desire, and pleasure."[4]

What absolute hogwash! This kind of nonsense is typical of self-serving C-Rock deception. First: There AREN'T any grey areas in the Bible! From Genesis to Revelation, God lays everything out in blacks and whites: Blessings/Cursings, Life/Death, Heaven/Hell, God/Satan, Christ/the world. Now make your choice. Why don't these supporters of "Christian" trash come clean and admit the obvious. If it sells, they'll sell it!

Anti-Rock minister Dr. Hal Webb put it better than I ever could:

> "When Christian music carries the beat, instrumentation, and exact sounds of the lost crowd, it results in confusion and shame... It is shameful to use musicians who in shallow songs daze instead of praise, who entertain instead of train... They transfer the worship owed to Christ to 'concert hopping', money-hungry entertainers who have never left the world far enough behind to stop sounding like it..."[5]

The final stop for stiff-necked C-Rock defenders is found here:

A HARDENED HEART AND SPIRIT

The angry, confused, denying and deluded C-Rock fan will always hit one final button as a last resort in his effort to justify his sin: It's called self-righteous pride:

> "I'm a Christian. I get good grades. I don't smoke. I don't drink. My parents are proud of me – and not one Bible verse says "Christian" Rock is wrong. I know what I'm doing and I don't see anything wrong with it."

Isaiah 64:6 says all our self-righteousness is a pile of dirty, stinking rags at God's feet. Yet C-Rock defenders continually justify their sin by patting their own backs. Noses in the air, they demand a scripture that says: "THUS SAITH THE LORD; THOU SHALT NOT LISTEN TO 'CHRISTIAN' ROCK". They overlook the fact the Bible also fails to specifically mention marijuana, cocaine, X-rated porno movies, and abortion as sins. Does that make them any less sinful?

Biblical holiness from Genesis to Revelation is swept under the rug by this kind of rock-hard, rebellious heart. C-Rock brainwashing has completed its task. The victim's rebellion is now set in concrete. Though living totally contrary to God's Word, the deluded, confused and hard-

19

hearted C-Rock victim prides himself in his "powerful" testimony for Jesus Christ.

But facts don't lie. The lives of hundreds of thousands of C-Rock fans are an ugly reflection of the face behind all "Christian" Rock.

It's called REBELLION!

2

What's Wrong With Hating The Church?

"Christian" Rock's position on the Church of the Lord Jesus Christ and traditional Church music can be summed up in one word:

CONTEMPT!

Masses of Christian youth and young adults greet traditional church music with a sneer, jeer and a snicker. God's not GOOD enough; the Church isn't SLICK enough; the music's not BAD enough, and Jesus isn't COOL enough! That's the message coming through loud and clear in the "Christian" Rock movement.

Though the C-Rock stars claim their purpose is to evangelize lost sinners, C-Rock's real purpose is two fold:

1.) To make their followers hate the traditional Church as much as they do.

2.) To breed rebellion, a refusal to submit to any type of authority.

These lyrics by CCM god Steve Taylor are a perfect example. Watch him heap scorching contempt on the Church Jesus Christ died for. His message is simple, "I will never submit to the authority of a church. I want to do things MY way."

I WANT TO BE A CLONE

"Be a clone and kiss conviction goodnight
　　Cloneliness is next to Godliness, right?
I'm grateful that they show the way
　　'Cause I could never know the way
To serve Him on my own, I want to be a clone...

So now I see the whole design
　　My church is an assembly line
The parts are there, I'm feeling fine
　　I want to be a clone.

I've learned enough to stay afloat
　　But not so much I rock the boat
I'm glad they shoved it down my throat
　　I want to be a clone.
Everybody must get cloned."

By the way, that final line is a tip of Taylor's hat to the famous Bob Dylan lyric, "Everybody must get STONED." Compare Steve's rebellious venom to what the BIBLE says:

> "They profess that they know God; but in works they deny him, being abominable, and disobedient, and unto every good work reprobate. But speak thou the things which become sound doctrine:"   Titus 1:16; 2:1

In churches all over the world, young believers are saying: "Man, let Grandma have that old boring junk. I'm not dead yet. I need something that MOVES me. I want some ROCK!"

If this is your attitude, then you don't really want true Christian music. Any old piece of worldly garbage will do, as long as you continue to get your Rock & Roll fix. Satan is in the excitement business, and if that's where your heart is, the devil has thrills, chills and spills by the truckload, as long as you keep dancing to HIS tune.

HAVE YOU BEEN SUCKED IN?

Are the grand old hymns of the faith a moldy slice of boring drivel to you? If so, you can be sure of two things:

1.) Carnal C-Rock propaganda has totally brainwashed your mind, and

2.) You're showing utter contempt for the richest wealth of scriptural music ever created.

The old hymns so despised by masses of bored

believers are so chock full of sound Bible, it makes the feeble attempts of today's CCM "stars" look like kindergarten show-and-tell.

Let's do a little comparison. Match the next two song lyrics against each other, and decide for yourself. Which one REALLY glorifies God?:

> "Holy, Holy, Holy!/ All the saints adore thee/ Casting down their golden crowns around the glassy sea/ Cherubim and seraphim falling down before Thee/ Who wert, and art, and evermore shalt be.
>
> Holy, Holy, Holy!/ Tho' the darkness hide thee/ Tho' the eye of sinful man Thy glory may not see/ Only Thou art holy/ There is none beside Thee/ Perfect in pow'r, in love, in purity..."

A generation raised on T.V., videos, Rock/Pop and other musical muck will look at those hymn stanzas and want to throw up.

"But I just don't UNDERSTAND that stuff," they'll complain. No wonder, it's all from the Bible. The great hymn writers of the past knew the Word of God! That's why their timeless words sound like a foreign language to today's lazy Laodiceans.

If this classic hymn was made into a C-Rock video, some hairy punk in a leather jacket and sunglasses would be butchering the words while the band bellowed behind him like a runaway freight train! But that's not likely, because few C-Rock fans could handle Bible theology as deep as the old classics. Here's the spiritual meat preferred now:

ROCK ON - Stryken

"Come on everybody/ Put your hands above your head/ Today we're screamin'/ 'Cause tomorrow you might be dead/ The earth is shakin', and the clouds are rolled away/ Come on everybody/ Get ready for the Judgment Day/ Rock on, Got my feet on the ground/ Got my eyes on Heaven/ Rock on..."

The classic Christian hymns are despised and hated for another gut-level reason: they don't feed our rotten flesh, they reveal it for what it really is, rotten to the core!

MY SAVIOUR'S LOVE

"I stand amazed in the presence of Jesus the Nazarene/ And wonder how He could love me/ A sinner condemned, unclean..."

Compare that piercing Bible truth to this bit of C-Rock wisdom, by CCM star Charlie Peacock:

BIG MAN'S HAT

"I used to have a big man's thoughts/ In a young man's world/ You got to have big man's thoughts/ To make a big man's girl/ And when I finally made that girl, she did not have a clue/ That I would break her like a matchstick/ That I could turn young love into the third world war..."

Who wants to hear about sin and redemption in Christian music when you can talk about your old girlfriends? Forget Jesus - let's communicate something REALLY important, like men and women's broken dreams.

Just to make sure we're socially relevant, let's throw in some pop psychology and a little unfulfilled teenage desire. And we'll do it all in the name of Christianity. What a bunch of self-serving slop.

IS YOUR MUSIC REALLY CHRISTIAN?

In short, you need to choose which side you're on. The C-Rock stars are telling you it's O.K. to call yourself a Christian, then mock everything Christ stands for. They are in for a big fall – and so are you if you continue following them.

You can't mock the Church Christ died for and expect God to bless you. Nor can you wallow in rebellious Rock music and expect to please God.

If you've been suckered into believing traditional church music is a load of old baloney, I urge you to repent before God and ask forgiveness for the sin of contempt. Mocking music that REALLY glorifies God stinks to high Heaven, and only a fool would try to get away with it.

God has ordained a certain kind of music for His

people and His Church. Here are a few ways you can tell:

- Music that uplifts The Church, rather than mocking and criticizing it.
- Music that carries Biblical messages, not anti-Biblical ones.
- Music that brings more glory to God than to the "star" who's performing.
- Music that feeds the spirit more than it feeds the rotten old flesh.

When you mock the Lord's music, the devil has you right where he wants you. Please don't make the mistake of sneering at godly music. If you do, the warning in this scripture will surely become your curse:

> "Be not deceived; God is not mocked: for whatsoever a man soweth, that shall he also reap."   Galatians 6:7

3

Is Music Really Neutral?

"We're like Billy Graham with guitars, basically...
rock and roll is neutral. It depends on the spirit."
Michael Bloodgood[1]

Today Satan is pushing a massive lie to deceive
and mislead multitudes of Christians. He has the
whole C-Rock industry barking on cue like trained
dogs. What are they saying?:

MUSIC IS NEUTRAL!

The neutrality of music is the root of the whole
C-Rock controversy. If music is neutral, then
anything goes. If not, then "Christian" Rock is a
farce, a fraud and a destructive force powerful
enough to blow churches apart.

Is music really neutral? The Biblical account of

David's playing which drove away Saul's evil spirit (1 Samuel 16:14-23) should bury that deception once and for all! Neutral music doesn't drive away demons, but David's music did. Yet many Christians today aren't satisfied with what the Bible says. They'd rather quench the Spirit, ignore the obvious, and buy the big lie. Why? To keep on sinning.

Let's use some common sense for a minute: If music is neutral, why did the thumping brass of that marching band at the football game make your pulse race? Why do they play that soothing Muzak in the dentist's office, if not to calm your nerves? And why did that passing car's blast of Heavy Metal noise make your heart pound?

The bottom line is: music is NEVER neutral! From barroom to church house, all music has some kind of positive or negative effect. Rock music is not neutral either. All Rock music promotes one thing: – animal lust:

> "But rock music has one appeal only, a barbaric appeal, to sexual desire – not love, not eros, but sexual desire undeveloped and untutored... Young people know that rock has the beat of sexual intercourse. That is why Ravel's Bolero is the one piece of classical music that is commonly known and liked by them..."[2]

> "....43 per cent of Americans past the age of 18 listen to music while making love. Pop music has long been concerned with love, if not lust.

Sometimes it has even crept into the classical repertoire. 'From the beginning to the end of its 339 measures,' wrote critic Edward Robinson four years after the 1928 debut of Ravel's Bolero, an orchestral piece that became a sensual standard, 'it is simply the incredible repetition of the same RHYTHM..."[3] (Emphasis author's).

ONLY THE LYRICS ARE IMPORTANT?

Many a CCM addict will violently disagree. They'll claim that even in Rock music, the MUSIC means nothing, only the LYRICS matter. Let's see.

No one can deny that the music of Elvis Presley and the *Beatles* sent millions of teenagers all over the world into sobbing, screaming, hysterical frenzies. If C-Rock's neutral philosophy is true, then that mob insanity surrounding Elvis and the *Beatles* was the result of their LYRICS, not their music. Here are the lyrics to two of the biggest hits Presley and the Fab Four ever produced:

TEDDY BEAR

"Just wanna be your teddy bear/ Don't wanna be a lion/ Cause lions play too rough/ Don't wanna be a tiger/ Cause tigers aren't the kind you love enough..."

I WANT TO HOLD YOUR HAND

"Oh yeah, I'll tell you somethin'/ I think you'll

understand/ When I say that somethin'/ I
wanna hold your hand..."

Sorry C-Rock fans, but those lyrics had nothing
to do with the mass hysteria surrounding Elvis
and the *Beatles*. Something MUCH bigger than
the dim-witted stanzas of Pop/Rock music turned
those little girls into screaming maniacs writhing
in a sexual frenzy. The power behind Presley
and the *Beatles'* success was made up of two
elements: The MUSIC and the spirit BEHIND the
music – the spirit of antichrist.

"Christian" Rock defenders say all music is neutral
and any kind of music can glorify God. Music
may be many things, but it is NEVER neutral.
Deep down inside, we all know this is true. Music
is a powerful spiritual creation that speaks directly
to our spirits. That's why Satan has infiltrated the
churches through C-Rock, so he can attack them
spiritually. MUSIC IS NOT NEUTRAL.

The following is taken from a poster CCM fans
are encouraged to order:

"THE CHRISTIAN ROCKER'S CREED"

"We hold these truths to be self-evident, that all
music was created equal that no instrument or
style of music is in itself evil - that the diversity
of musical expression which flows forth from
man is but one evidence of the boundless creativity
of our Heavenly Father..."[4]

Isn't it interesting, advocates of homosexual churches say the same thing! Fill in the blanks with any pet sin, and you'll see the message behind this declaration of independence loud and clear:

> **"LEAVE MY SIN ALONE!** I can't live without it, but it doesn't affect me!"

Christian writer Dr. David Noebel says:

> "It is difficult to comprehend how Christian musicians can talk about new creation, new life in Christ, resurrection values, righteousness and purity and proceed to wrap these lofty and spiritual concepts and values into a neo-pagan, primitive, rhythmic, atheistic musical style copied directly from those who have declared war on these very values... Christian rock groups have brought into the church a music reflecting man's warfare against God. Modern art, literature, films and music are all conveying this message. By accepting modern rock into the church we are party to the destruction of the very values we say we expound..."[5]

WHAT IS CHRISTIAN MUSIC?

Christian music is music about JESUS CHRIST. The focus of real Christian songs isn't on dope, abortion, starvation or self-esteem. Let the world debate worldly problems; the Christian is supposed to have his eyes fixed on Jesus! (Hebrews 12:1,2 and Colossians 3:2-4). And we're not talking about some cardboard cut-out Christ who loves

32

all and judges none, either. That kind of Jesus sells lots of tapes, but exists only in the minds of the deluded and deceived.

If you take Jesus Christ out of the music, it's no more "Christian" than the man in the moon. Just because some famous name sings about peer pressure doesn't make him or his music "Christian." When the Lord is forced to take a back seat to the world's garbage dump, that music's not about Jesus; it's about the singer's pet projects. There's a word for this phenomenon. It's called PRIDE.

One of the most common pieces of mail I receive from hot C-Rock fans is the famous tract by Keith Green called "Can God Use Rock Music?" It's no wonder multitudes of Christians blindly believe the "music is neutral" lie. The biggest names in the industry all preach the same thing!

The fans have become so thoroughly brainwashed by their CCM gods, they can only repeat the same line over and over again – "Music is neutral... Music is neutral... Music is neutral..." Where did they first learn this nonsense? From Keith Green:

> "But ALL the examples I mentioned above have to do with the motives of the heart, NOT the music itself! That is why I believe that music, in itself, is a neutral force. Let me give you a better example.

> Take a knife for instance. With it, you can cut bread, carve a roast, loose someone who's been bound by ropes, or you can do harm and even kill somebody. In other words, you can be destructive and murderous. The knife itself, when put in an atmosphere of hoodlums, becomes a weapon. But put it in a kitchen, and it becomes a tool that's useful, even necessary, for the preparation of nourishment for your family..."[6]

Though his sincerity cannot be questioned, Keith Green made a major mistake when he wrote those words. The "neutrality" of music is a slick lie and a sick joke. A knife is a dead piece of steel, but music has a life of its own! Rock music has proven itself to be a satanic force powerful enough to lead millions into rebellion.

Blinded by his own involvement in "Christian" Rock, Green promoted a deception that has spread like wildfire. His tract is a handy excuse used by multitudes to do one thing – keep feeding their flesh.

Keith Green makes another amazing statement in this same tract. If he had lived long enough to see the rotten, abominable "fruit" of all Rock music today, he'd surely have changed his tune:

> "The suggestion that there is such a thing as intrinsically 'good music' or 'evil music' seems preposterous to me. I have been involved with almost every aspect of music my whole life, and I have witnessed the various effects it has had

> on me and other people – and I have to say that
> I have never ONCE seen a case where music was
> the DIRECT CAUSE OF SIN OR WICKEDNESS
> IN A PERSON'S LIFE."[7]

Did you catch that? Keith Green, the father of modern C-Rock, is saying that NO music is "intrinsically evil." That means the brain-pounding noise spewed out by Heavy Metal bands who openly praise and worship Satan isn't really evil– and it doesn't cause any sin in a person's life! How many thousands of naive young Christians have bought Green's bunk during the past ten years? Plenty.

Keith evidently wasn't aware that an ENTIRE GENERATION'S sin was the direct result of the music they worshiped! Where'd the smoke-dope philosophy come from, if not through the "music" of monsters like the *Beatles*, *Stones*, *Dead* and *Who*? Crack cocaine hit the ghettoes and high-rises of 1980's America like a ton of bricks because the foundation was laid a decade earlier by the drug-peddling, pill-popping 60's super-Rockers.

Where'd the occultism and Hindu junk of today's New Age explosion come from, if not the "music" produced by witchy bands like *Jefferson Airplane*, Hendrix and the *Doors*? The spirit of the 60's is still alive and well in the 90's – it's the spirit of REBELLION. Want to find the root of our society's destruction? It's in the "music" of radical 60's anarchists like *Steppenwolf*, Bob Dylan and John

Lennon. Wherever you find drugs, rebellion and chaos, you'll find Rock music floating just beneath the surface.

Rock music is wrong because Rock & Roll has been based on rebellion from the start, and there's no such thing as good rebellion (1 Samuel 15:23). In CCM music, this fact is quickly swept under the carpet and buried. By definition, "neutral" music could never produce negative results. If 25 years of Rock-related wickedness hasn't taught us that, then we're beyond teaching.

IS IT EVEN MUSIC?

Incidentally, Rock "music" isn't even music. It's noise! *Rolling Stone* Mick Jagger admitted it. Why won't the "Christian" Rockers?:

> "It's a noise we make. That's all. You could be kind and call it music."[8]

In his excellent book, "Face the Music - Contemporary Church Music On Trial," author Lenny Seidel sets the record straight. A concert pianist and twenty-five year Christian music veteran, Seidel proves beyond a shadow of a doubt that music is about as "neutral" as a black eye. Lenny brings out the following points:

> "True godly music will be composed of three elements – all in perfect balance with each other. They are: MELODY, HARMONY, and RHYTHM.

> Rock "music" has no melody - only fragments of
> melody endlessly repeated. Since there is no true
> melody, there is no real harmony. There is only
> rhythm. And rhythm in and of itself is not music."[9]

Seidel also points out that true godly music will
come to a definite resolution. Does Rock, Pop and
"Christian" Rock fit this guideline? Are you
kidding? The average Rock song ends one of two
ways: with a crash that sounds like someone just
pulled the plug, or a day-long fade-out.

Many a diehard C-Rocker will scream, "All that's
just your opinion. I don't agree with any of it!"
That's fine, but you have just thrown out hundreds
of years of musical culture. It's kind of like trading
a sirloin steak for a Big Mac and swearing you
got the best part of the deal!

NEUTRAL FORCES DON'T DESTROY!

The rhythms (not the words) of Rock music have
been PROVEN to cause brain damage in laboratory
animals.[10] Does this sound like a "neutral" force?

Rock music has been PROVEN to kill plants. Is
killing living organisms neutral?[11]

The stopped anapestic beat of Rock & Roll has
been PROVEN to instantly sap physical strength
from the listener.[12] Doesn't sound neutral to me.

Rock music has been PROVEN to have a

detrimental effect on the adrenaline, sex glands and blood sugar of the human brain.[13] Study after study has shown that Rock music ALWAYS stunts growth and chokes off life. Are death and destruction neutral? Come on.

Any "Christian" Rock star/fan who thinks music is neutral should face up to one simple fact: nobody gets hooked on neutral music. Why don't you do a little experiment? Spend the next 30 days without listening to or playing ANY rock music. (Six months would be better).

Try it, C-Rock fans. You'll quickly find yourself going through WITHDRAWAL, because Rock music is a DRUG! Don't believe it? Go 30 days without it.

Here's some technical information you need:

<u>MELODY</u>

True melodic formula (motive) will combine to create phrases and themes, each individual melody having its own contour of ascending and descending pitches. There will be a definite high place near the conclusion, showing proper resolution. Static movement and lack of balance will create either a hypnotic effect or despair in the listener.[14] Based on these guidelines, Rock "music" has no melody at all.

HARMONY

"All harmony is based on chordal patterns which support the melody subserviently. Chords are based on a very specific keynote, or tonic, and must move through prescribed formulas in the traditional harmonic structure of the major-minor tonal system.

The modulation of keys, as charted on the Circle of Fifths, will show great regularity in the relationships of chords, pitches, scales, and tonalities. Excessive consonance and/or dissonance will not be evident."[15] Based on these guidelines, Rock "music" has no harmony.

RHYTHM

Rhythm is the orderly movement of music through time. Constant alternation of triple and duple measures creates a driving syncopation, producing excessive tension. Subtle balance between regular accent patterns and occasional syncopation is necessary to avoid hypnotic effect. (There's that nasty word "effect" again.)

Based on these guidelines, Rock "music's" rhythm is a combination of unending backbeats and breakbeats whose ultimate end is to swamp the listener and totally consume them in an intense artificial atmosphere of dominance. This should never be the intent of rhythm.[16]

PITCH

True music has a variety of pitches which are ACCURATE. Very high pitches are used only for contrast and climax points. Rock music is just the opposite. Its constant repetition of pitches almost never modulates, and is slightly UNDER true pitch (as in "Blues"). The high pitched screams, both human and electronic, are thrown helter-skelter throughout, the end result being musical chaos.[17]

INTENSITY

True music employs much contrast between loud and soft, with a constant change in the dynamic level. There is always a wide, CONTROLLED variation in qualitative force intensity. Rock "music" has an intensity that is as loud as possible – as long as possible. The dynamic has all the subtlety of a freshly detonated neutron bomb.[18]

The end result: ROCK MUSIC IS NOT EVEN MUSIC. Where does this leave "Christian" Rock music?: "CHRISTIAN" ROCK MUSIC IS NOT EVEN MUSIC.

Where does this leave CCM music? CCM covers a wide range of musical styles, but MOST of it is Rock, and Rock is not music; it's noise. Add it all up, and here's what you've got: Christians are trying to spread the Gospel of Jesus Christ through a musical medium which doesn't even exist.

Secondly, there is no such thing as "Christian" Rock, for Rock "music" is the exact opposite of everything Jesus Christ stands for.

Noise is still noise no matter how its packaged, sold, accepted or defended. The medium of chaos doesn't fit the message of the Bible, leaving the listener and (musician) in confusion, deception and one monster of a spiritual mess. Flesh and spirit cannot operate together, as the Holy Spirit through the Apostle Paul brought out so well in Galatians 5:16,17:

> "This I say then, Walk in the Spirit, and ye shall not fulfil the lust of the flesh. For the flesh lusteth against the Spirit, and the Spirit against the flesh: and these are contrary the one to the other; so that ye cannot do the things that ye would."

Do you really want to serve the Lord Jesus Christ with all your heart, mind, soul and strength? Then dump "Christian" Rock.

These next two excerpts are from letters concerned Christians have sent me. These are just two of the many people who understand that "Christian" Rock music is NOT neutral, and never has been. Read and heed these comments from people who have seen C-Rock from the inside-out:

41

"This generation says 'Jesus Christ rocks.' What is the next generation going to say that Jesus Christ does?... Christian rock may win a few converts by the grace of God, especially if it is true that many of its performers are true Christians with good intentions and they use His Word. But in the end we will pollute and confuse and deceive almost the entire next generation of the Body of Christ.

Christian rock is helping to change the image of God into something vulgar, created by or at least copied from the imaginations of our twentieth century rebellious human mind, which glorifies self rather than God..."[19]

"'...an epidemic of unreason.' Is this not what you see at a rock concert? Has not this Black Magic called Contemporary Gospel-rock music, caused a great falling away from the precepts of a God Who Is The Same Yesterday and Today? Has the Bible said, 'Thou shalt be liberal in the 1980's?' Does rock music not instill rebellion? Is not rebellion as the sin of WITCHCRAFT?...

What in the world are these Christians doing practicing Black Magic today! Is not rock music and Black Magic one and the same? Need I say more to prove this? What? You mean HIS children still have not decided whom they are going to worship? You mean the prophets of Baal still exist in their lives? Surely you jest! So let's end all of these Rock music exposes'. Surely they are not that willingly ignorant... Are they?"[20]

42

4

Christian Rock
Is Satan's Seat

"I know thy works, and where thou dwellest,
even where Satan's seat is:... But I have a
few things against thee, because thou hast
there them that hold the doctrine of Balaam,
who taught Balac to cast a stumblingblock
before the children of Israel, to eat things
sacrificed unto idols, and to commit
fornication." Revelation 2:13,14

Witchcraft and New Ageism are now a basic part
of Christian Contemporary Music. By apeing every
aspect of their worldly counterparts, the C-Rock
stars have followed them straight down the same
deadly path to Satan's front door. Though they
won't admit it, they're ringing the devil's doorbell
in the name of Jesus!

Since C-Rockers are copying their secular

counterparts, they must contend that secular Rock is NOT demonic. If they admit it is, they'd have a problem promoting demonic Christian music.

Unfortunately, they are fighting a losing battle. First-hand testimony from former satanist Mike Warnke in his book "The Satan-Seller" proves the connection between Rock music and satanism:

> "I had planned on using acid rock to keep our young crowd tuned in... We had initiated hypnotic rock music as a prelude to our rituals and encouraged heavier usage of drugs to get with it."[1]

ROCK STARS ADMIT IT

The elder statesmen of secular Rock have bragged about the demonics behind their music again and again. Here are just two examples:

> "My true belief about Rock 'n' Roll - and there have been a lot of phrases attributed to me over the years - is this: I believe this kind of music is demonic....A lot of the beats in music today are taken from voodoo, from the voodoo drums. If you study music in rhythms, like I have, you'll see that is true...." - Little Richard[2]

> "It [the Bible] says make merry with the joy of God only. But when it comes to WORLDLY music, rock 'n' roll.... Man, I got THE DEVIL in me! If I didn't have, I'd be a Christian.... Cause I'm

draggin' the audience to hell with me. How am I gonna git 'em to heaven with 'Whole Lotta Shakin' Goin' On'? You can't serve two masters; you'll hate one an' love the other." - Jerry Lee Lewis[3]

Blinded heads in the sand, most C-Rock fans deny the obvious – that secular Rock is inspired, controlled and manipulated by demons. They HAVE to say that, or they'll be forced to pitch their C-Rock into the nearest trash can. Pro-CCM spokesman Al Menconi defines the hypocrisy:

"The music is inspired by demons... First, where did he get this information? It's news to me. I study the same Bible he does, as well as the Satanic Bible, occult and ritual books – everything I can get my hands on relating to the subjects of music and the occult. I've never found this mentioned or even hinted at in any way..."[4]

Mike Warnke, Little Richard, Jerry Lee Lewis and countless others say otherwise, and they've all been on the INSIDE of Satan's cage.

Let's examine some CCM stars. A musical style isn't the only thing they've brought home from the devil's crowd. When Rock started wearing the label "Christian," Satan moved right in. We know because Lucifer's fingerprints are all over C-Rock music.

Does this mean all the CCM stars mentioned are

Devil-worshipers? No. Only God knows their heart (Jeremiah 17:9,10). But one thing's for sure: Satan's mark is on this stuff because these "Christian" Rockers and CCMers are in the devil's musical territory, whether they know it or not. By trying to use Satan's filth for God's glory, they have left themselves wide open to deception, confusion and a swamp of spiritual delusion.

Figure 1

Figure 1 is the flip side of the "Big Picture" record album. Notice how Michael W. Smith's name is written – backwards.

Writing reversal is a SATANIC principle. Master satanist Aleister Crowley taught his disciples to walk backwards, talk backwards, think backwards, speak backwards, write backwards and even listen to phonograph records backwards to gain insight into the future.

The "M" and the "T" in Michael and Smith are part of a satanic writing called the RUNIC alphabet. According to World Book Encyclopedia, the very name "Rune" means "secret." These symbols were so connected with witchcraft, the early Christian missionaries in Europe refused to use them. They replaced this satanic sign language with the Latin alphabet instead.[5]

Packages on display in the New Age section of many mall bookstores detail the ancient occult practice of "casting the runes," using these signs.

Does this make Michael W. Smith a satanist? No. Without a doubt, he has written some of the most beautiful praise choruses to be sung in many a year. Like all CCMers, however, Michael W. Smith is a product of an INDUSTRY, the "Christian" Rock industry. Any industry ultimately translates down to one thing, the dollar sign.

47

Many involved in CCM may be trying to serve the Lord with all their heart, mind, soul and strength, but they are told, "You've got contracts. You've got commitments. You'd better soften up the preaching in that last batch of songs, before you 'turn people off.' If you don't play the game by our rules, your sales will slip and you won't be able to 'minister' to as many souls."

Here's the bottom line: Michael W. Smith has the same choice as all CCMers – stay in a compromised industry, or get out. Obviously, he chose to stay in, and Satan has marked him for it.

Figure 2

48

Figure 2 is from an album by CCM stars *Glad*. Look carefully into the distance behind the band and you will notice two things: 1.) They're not really standing on a roadway; it's a pyramid! and 2.) The apex of that pyramid is being hit by a lightning bolt.

Figure 3

The pyramid has been a standard of witchcraft and occultic power for centuries. And Satan has used the lightning strike as his own personal calling card throughout secular Rock albums for years. Now he's marking his territory in "Christian" Rock as well (See Luke 10:18).

Match the *Glad* photo against Figure 3, "Powerslave," by Heavy Metal Satan-Rockers, *Iron Maiden*. The cover art's theme is identical to *Glad's*. The peak of the pyramid is crawling with lightning bolts, the power of Lucifer striking the heart of the New Age.

Those deceived by CCM will argue, "Big deal. That doesn't mean anything." It may mean nothing to YOU, but it sure is important to those who designed those album covers! In the occult, symbolism, logos and witchcraft signs are a very big deal indeed. The powers behind these groups don't spend hundreds of hours and thousands of dollars making up meaningless projects.

IN GOD WE TRUST – *STRYPER* (See Figure 4).

Masses of CCM fans are so thoroughly *Stryper*-ized by the yellow and black attack, they refuse to face facts. How could anything possibly be wrong with these C-Rocking pretty boys? After all, they DO talk about God. Why, they even dump Bibles on their fans like red-hot concert souvenirs. Too bad their fans drop them in the dirt afterwards:

> "*Stryper* are rumored to spend $1,000 a night on the Bibles, and cleaners of stadiums in the U.S.

have complained about having to sweep up piles of the tomes left by rock fans who would probably rather read 'Metal' magazine..."[6]

Figure 4

If *Stryper* ever read the Bibles they cast into the dust, they'd see what an abomination it was:

> "Give not that which is holy unto the dogs, neither cast ye your pearls before swine, lest

51

> they trample them under their feet, and
> turn again and rend you."   Matthew 7:6

Since pitching Bibles like baseballs didn't work,
Stryper hit on a sure-fire plan for outdoor concerts
– dump 'em on the crowd like water balloons!

> "WORD FROM ON HIGH – God Rockers *Stryper*,
> touring America's open-air venues, have hired a
> helicopter to drop copies of the Bible on their
> fans. At some bigger shows they've dropped
> 10,000 and at 8 pounds a copy that eats up the
> profits. It can't be much fun for the fan who gets
> hit on the head. But that's a cross they have to
> bear!"[7]

I wonder how many *Stryper* fans know about the
blatant occultism splashed all over their records,
tapes, CDs, uniforms, videos and stage show.
The satanic spirit controlling this group was
thoroughly documented in "DANCING WITH
DEMONS". But now there's much more to expose.

We showed in "DANCING" that on the inner
sleeve of their "To Hell With The Devil" album,
Stryper guitarist Oz Fox sported a digital phrase
on his chest that read "DIMENSION 4." One hot
Stryper fan told me Dimension 4 represented a
guitar effects pedal! Read this quote about the
new designer drug "ICE" to get the real story:

> "Dr. Alex Stalcup, medical director at the Haight-
> Ashbury free clinic, has dealt with a half-dozen
> persons lapsed into ice psychosis. 'I was just

talking to one guy who was on ice and had a
gate somewhere in his apartment that was open
and was letting in demons from the Fourth
Dimension - whatever that is - and he couldn't
close it.'"[8]

In "DANCING" we also detailed the significance
of the 777 *Stryper* says is a godly alternative to
the antichrist's 666. Actually, it's a master numeric
in satanism, and is the title of a book by Devil-
worshiper Aleister Crowley! (See Figure 5).

Figure 5

The next photo of *Stryper* was taken before they were *Stryper*. (See Figure 6).

Figure 6

This picture is from a California music paper called BAM. That's Michael and Robert Sweet in the background. The date is August 13, 1982. *Stryper's* conversion to Christ supposedly took place in 1983.[9] *Stryper's* first album, "Yellow & Black Attack," wasn't released until 1984.

At the top of the picture are two sets of "777" prominently displayed. This ad was done a year before *Stryper* claims to have gotten saved! If that's a godly number NOW, why were they using it back then? The triple 7 has always been the satanist's number. And yellow and black are considered the "livery" (uniform) of the Devil.[10]

Let's get this straight: before they were saved, *Stryper* wore the devil's uniform, used the devil's number and sang the devil's music. And now they want us to believe they are serving God without changing any of it?

Some *Stryper*-ized fan is sure to say, "That's impossible! *Stryper* would never do anything to bring shame to Jesus." If that's you, keep reading.

In 1989 *Stryper* toured with secular Rockers *White Lion*. Their drummer, Greg D'Angelo, reveals a few of the God Squad's antics:

> "The last night of the tour, we were in Milwaukee and had a whole floor of the hotel. We threw a party and invited about 150 fans. We filled up a bathtub with beer and champagne. The *Stryper* guys came, and we were having a great time rolling in the aisles and chasing skirts! About two in the morning Robert Sweet was whacked! Drunk! He had on his customized blue, bug-eye Porsche sunglasses and was being dragged around on his tiptoes by two women holding him up!"[11]

THE REAL FRUIT

For those who doubt this information, the real

fruit of *Stryper's* "ministry" is in their fans. For a good look at the wicked spirit driving this group, check out this letter from a *Stryper*-ized Metalhead, taken from CREEM METAL magazine, May, 1987, pgs. 59,60:

> "First, please publish my letter. Thanks!! Second: This letter goes to that screwed up !@#$%, Thrasher of Brentwood, MD. I read your stupid letter about callin' *Stryper* "fags." *Stryper* is the ultimate. See, you like your !@#$% up bands like *Slayer*, D.R.I. and Exodus. Those !@#$% have stuff that have to do with satanic !@#$%. *Stryper* is here to tell the world of Jesus Christ. They're on a mission from God. They have nothing to do with Hell or Satan. So here's my two points; 1) *Stryper* rules, and 2) you can take your bands and shove them up your !@#$%.
> Isaiah 53:5
> Bethlehem, PA
> P.S. And as the rest of you fags who hate *Stryper*: go to Hell with the Devil. I love METAL magazine."

There's plenty of sparkling, holy, godly fruit in THAT *Stryper* fan! Even non-Christians have better spiritual discernment, as these excerpts show, taken from the same letters page in CREEM METAL magazine:

> "... You don't - repeat - don't mix religion and rock 'n' roll! Rock is about the Devil and darkness, while God is good and light. Right or wrong?
> A *Stryper* Hater
> Concord, NH"

56

"... Face it: religion and metal just don't mix!
Never have and NEVER will...
#1 Iron Maiden fan!
E.S.
Jensen Beach, FL"

Sin always finds out the sinner (Numbers 32:23), and *Stryper* finally dropped their mask. A money-making mass of hypnotized fans solidly under their belt, the *Stryper* boys no longer feel the need to be so "radical" in their Christianity. They know enough people have now been conditioned to keep handing over bucks for *Stryper* product, no matter what. Here's proof:

"...You won't pick up this record ("Against The Law") and hear anything that says 'God' or 'Christ'. That was intentionally done. We were tired of people coming back with excuses, saying 'Sorry we can't play this.' MTV's got to play this and the radio's got to play it or it doesn't serve the purpose..." [12] Robert Sweet

CCM magazine threw their two cents in:

"Everybody's talking about *Stryper's* recent interviews in secular magazines, where they talk about a new direction with their music and their lyrics. The band responds to those questioning their faith by saying that their goal is still 'to be a band of great rock and roll musicians who live by Christian beliefs.' They desire to write some lyrics for their next album that aren't necessarily about God in every song: the goal being top 40 radio airplay..."[13]

57

And all this time I thought the goal was to win lost Rock fans to Christ. Funny how things change, isn't it?

Stryper drummer Robert Sweet has an interesting personal testimony about how he found Christ:

> "I was basically the same guy as far as the way I look now. But, I hadn't really given my life to God... (Being a Christian) doesn't necessarily mean that you become this type of religious person and you change the way you look etc. You can do that if you want, but it is not a priority..."[14]

Accepting Christ without total change in your life is a comforting thought to sinners who want to have their cake and eat it too. The Bible puts salvation in a little different light, though:

> "Therefore if any man be in Christ, he is a new creature: old things are passed away; behold, all things are become new."
> 2 Corinthians 5:17

Not some. Not most. ALL.

Stryper guitarist Michael Sweet's personal testimony is even more disturbing:

> "Well, my story is a little different. There wasn't anything certain that made me want to have Christ in my life..."[15]

If this statement is true, then Michael Sweet isn't even saved! The realization of our own SIN is what drives people to make Jesus Christ their Saviour:

> "But God commendeth his love toward us, in that, while we were yet sinners, Christ died for us. Much more then, being now justified by his blood, we shall be saved from wrath through him."   Romans 5:8,9

Realizing and acting on this is called REPENTANCE. Without it, no one can be saved, much less lead others into the Kingdom!

> "I tell you, Nay: but, except ye repent, ye shall all likewise perish."   Luke 13:5

When hit with hard truth like this, the confused CCM fan usually asks, "How is this possible? How could SATAN be using something dedicated to God?" The answer is very simple. Rock music BELONGS to Satan, and God wants nothing to do with it, no matter who dedicates it to Him.

Rock & Roll is the devil's perversion of a powerful creation of God – music. If you're open to receiving the spiritual truth behind that statement, you will see Satan's footprints all over modern Contemporary Christian Music. Let's match the Bible against reality.

Satan is pride personified (Isaiah 14:12-15). The

proud, ungodly Pharisees of Jesus' day were the epitome of Luciferian conceit in action. They blew trumpets before them, and loved the praise of men for their good deeds (Matthew 6:1,2,5).

When it comes to wanting attention, the "Christian" Rockers are second to none. Besides soaking up praise and worship at concerts and personal appearances, they roll out the T-shirts, headbands, buttons, album covers and every other trinket imaginable bearing their images.

But even that isn't enough. They also use all their pet social causes (feeding the hungry, teen problems, the environment and one-worldism) to gain even more limelight. Everything they do is geared toward getting all eyes on THEM.

Lucifer CRAVES worship (Luke 4:5-7). And so do the "Christian" Rockers. Here's an example, from Mick Rowe and his C-Metal band *Tempest*:

IN HIS NAME (ROCK ON)

"When you hear our music being played/ Do you like the sound of my scream/ When Mick plays his electric guitar/ Do you like the volume of his lead/ Rock on with Jesus he's the one/ Rock on with Jesus he's the son/ Rock on with Jesus and you'll never be the same/ Rock on with me in his name..."

Tempest singer J.R. Rowe's proud lyrics make him

sound like Jesus Christ's hard-Rockin' RIGHT-HAND MAN! Any true Christian will be thoroughly disgusted by such shameless, prideful peacocking. Some C-Rock fan will fire back, "But he talked about Jesus, didn't he?" Study your Bible and you'll find that the devil talked a great deal about the Lord too. Does that make him a Christian?

WHO RECEIVES THE WORSHIP?

What about the milder side of the coin, those laid-back, squeaky-clean CCM superstars who inspire such frenzy at their live shows? Who is REALLY being worshiped? The fans all deny idolatry, but these quotes from a Reunion Records promo for Michael W. Smith's "Big Picture" tour tell the real story:

> "Smith, with synthesizers blaring, drums blazing, and guitars screeching, sent a young crowd into a frenzy from beginning to end." – Richard Linihan, Tulsa Tribune

> "With sweeping strobes lighting the stage and crowd areas, Smith took the stage with some twirling dance steps that sent the crowd into rocking frenzy. The moment Smith's hands hit the air, the audience responded with over-the-head hand claps and stomping feet." – Merle Havenga, Grand Rapids Press

If that's not worship, what is? And there's no

question who's being worshiped. Where was Jesus Christ in all that hoopla?

Even though fans and stars will deny it to the death, the focus of worship at C-Rock concerts is NOT the Lord Jesus Christ. If it was, there'd be no need for light shows, fog banks, wild music and super-slick production numbers guaranteed to whip people's emotions to a peak. Jesus Christ needed no gimmicks to draw men to Him (John 2:24,25 & 18:20,21). If the Lord Jesus Christ is not being worshiped, then who is?

Whether they know it or not, the crowd is really worshiping the demons who fuel the whole show. Don't believe it? Consider the following facts:

SPIRITUAL FRENZY

Look at the reaction of the fans, especially the women, at CCM concerts. C-Rock kings *Stryper* have stated they don't give altar calls because the crowd might mob them and rip their clothes off![16] This should tell you what kind of spirit is let loose at those shows. It's certainly not the same spirit found in John 12:32:

> "And I, if I be lifted up from the earth, will draw all men unto me"

Still wonder which spirit is leading *Stryper?* Read this account from an Australian newspaper about a "God-Squad" fan who nearly got his arm cut off during the group's appearance at a record store:

> "Robert [Sweet] was visiting two *Stryper* fans injured on Saturday when they were pushed through a plate glass window as more than 1500 enthusiasts tried to meet the band members at a record store... 'I thought my arm had been cut off', Michael [Squier] said. 'There was blood everywhere and someone had to hold it together... three veins were cut...' "[17]

Take a close look at Sweet's compassionate comments about his fans' mutilation:

> "What happened on Saturday was purely rock and roll. It shows we're not wimpy religious Christian guys, but a real rock and roll venture. Robert said the band had never experienced complete hysteria like they witnessed on Saturday and were sorry people got hurt, but *Stryper* still 'don't mind people being wild'..."[18]

Did you catch that? Robert Sweet was actually PROUD it happened because this proved *Stryper* weren't "religious wimps." His "concern" for this sliced-up fan was used to show everyone just how macho *Stryper* really are.

The evil spirit behind that rabid record store frenzy is perfectly described in 2 Timothy 3:4-7. *Stryper* - take a look in the mirror:

> "Traitors, heady, highminded, lovers of

> "Traitors, heady, highminded, lovers of pleasures more than lovers of God; Having a form of godliness, but denying the power thereof: from such turn away. For of this sort are they which creep into houses, and lead captive silly women laden with sins, led away with divers lusts, Ever learning, and never able to come to the knowledge of the truth."

God has made it clear in His Word that He will have nothing to do with a dirty vessel (2 Timothy 2:20,21). Yet the same wild, worldly spirit that lost sinners love so much also fuels the C-Rock shows. How?

What about the masses of people swaying, screaming and worshiping before the altar (the stage) as these groups crank it up? What about the Christian Punk "moshers" slam-dancing for Jesus, just like their lost counterparts do at the secular Rock orgies? How does activity like that match up against Romans 12:2?

> "And be not conformed to this world: but be ye transformed by the renewing of your mind, that ye may prove what is that good, and acceptable, and perfect will of God."

IDOLATRY

Fans so idolize their C-Rock gods, they become mesmerized by even the names and slogans of these groups. The fans soak them up like water, then spit them out again - sayings like: "Holy Thrash," "God's Speed," "God Rules" and "Jesus Christ Rocks."

"David banged his head, so why can't I?" they growl, with a defiant sneer. Their T-shirts tell the real story, overpriced souvenirs plastered with the gaudy names, phrases and logos of C-Rock gods. The fans can deny their idolatry all they want, but paying $30 for a cheap T-shirt and glossy concert program is still worship any way you slice it. That's because Rock music and all that goes with it is a RELIGION, Satan's religion.

Revelation 21:8 says no idolator will enter into the Kingdom of Heaven, and Galatians 4:9 lays C-Rock idolatry right on the line:

> "But now, after that ye have known God, or rather are known of God, how turn ye again to the weak and beggarly elements whereunto ye desire again to be in bondage?"

Does Satan really control "Christian" Rock? Take a look at these lyrics, and ask yourself: Who gets the glory, Jesus or Lucifer?:

FEAR NO EVIL - Messiah Prophet Band

"Racing along at break neck speed/ Running for your life/ Wolves have bared their teeth again/ The moon shines full tonight/ You see their faces twist and turn/ The creatures of the

night/ Bloody hands and blood-stained fangs/
Challenge you to fight.."

And that is supposed to be Christian? Sorry. This
music has "Satan" written all over it. Here's what
the whole mess adds up to:

- **Satan is the god of Rock.**

- **Rock music is a dirty vessel God
  refuses to use.**

- **Many Christians could care less.**

The only question left is: Are you one of them? If
so, *WHY?*

5

What's Wrong With New Age Teaching in CCM?

Has the New Age gained a stranglehold on Contemporary Christian Music today? You bet it has; the fans just don't realize it yet. When confronted with the ugly truth, they'll say, "Not the stuff I listen to... No way."

Don't be so sure. Satan is doing his best to cover ALL musical bases with his lies and deceitful manipulation. Why? To prepare the world for the antichrist system. (Incidentally, antichrist and the New Age are the same thing).

In his excellent book "Ravaged By the New Age", Christian author Texe Marrs defined the movement this way - "ANYTHING BUT JESUS".[1]

In the New Age religion, a generic Jesus is fine and dandy. A human Jesus is o.k. too. In fact, ANYTHING goes, spiritually speaking, except the hard, straight, narrow account of Jesus Christ of Nazareth, the Only Begotten Son of God.

Very few Christians are musically selective when it comes to their favorite stars. To spot Satan's subtle schemes and scams, we MUST test everything, hold onto the good, and pitch the rest (1 Thessalonians 5:21).

How does New Age deception apply to CCM? Take a look at this quote by C-Rock star Dana Key:

> "What's strange about the New Age is that it has several things in common with Christianity. It wants to deal with the world's problems and increase people's self-esteem, which I think Christianity has an interest in as well..."[2]

Key's statement *IS* New Age! Are we really supposed to believe that Christianity has several things in common with antichrist? The Aquarian gurus behind the movement say we are all gods; we just haven't discovered our divinity yet. The Bible has NOTHING in common with that mess!

> "In the sweat of thy face shalt thou eat bread, till thou return unto the ground; for out of it wast thou taken: for dust thou art, and unto dust shalt thou return."
>
> Genesis 3:19

68

Also, when did Jesus Christ ever seek to increase people's self-esteem? Certainly not in THIS Scripture:

> "Fill ye up then the measure of your fathers. Ye serpents, ye generation of vipers, how can ye escape the damnation of hell?"
>
> Matthew 23:32,33

Increasing self-esteem used to be called plain old PRIDE. And God hates it (Obadiah 3,4 & Proverbs 16:18,19). The only thing the New Age and Christianity have in common are the CCMers promoting the devil's New Age ideas through their music and interviews!

As masses of people fall away from the tough path of following a holy Lord, religious music naturally apes the trend. Most CCM will always chase the dollars, as the past ten years have clearly shown. If it's popular, they want a piece of it. Forget scripture – anything goes, as long as it's "kind of Christian."

A good example of this is secular Rock superstars, *U2*, a favorite with Christian youth everywhere because lead singer Bono Hewson is supposed to be born-again. Carnal Christians continue playing this game of flesh-feeding because *U2's* music is so "spiritual." Is *U2* really a Christian band? Let's hear it from the lips of Bono himself:

> "We live in a culture where people literally worship the material world. We're brought up to denigrate pagan cultures that worship the sun and moon - yet we worship this little round silver thing, the coin. Myself, I prefer to worship the moon..."[3]

"But surely that statement was tongue-in-cheek," *U2* fans will argue. Read on to see what kind of "Christian" Bono really is:

> "...Bono dislikes the label 'born-again Christian' - and he doesn't go to church either. 'I'm a very, very bad advertisement for God...'"[4]

Here's how "born-again" Bono lets off steam:

> "Born again Christian Bono has slipped from his saintly ways - with a nine-hour binge which left him 'brainless'... The U2 star... got stuck into beer, wine, cocktails and bubbly celebrating the American release of the band's Rattle And Hum film. 'He was slobbering, shouting and showing off', said a bartender at the Santa Monica niterie that hosted the bash. 'Even the rest of the band told him to calm down. They should have been kicked out but because of who they are we let them stay...'"[5]

YESTERDAY'S GARBAGE– TODAY'S RELIGION

New Age influence in CCM is subtle and

spreading. Deception is the name of the game, and the New Agers have a dozen ways to play it. One favorite trick is to refry a rusty old secular tune, then bring it back out as "Christian." (*Petra* paved the way years ago, by remaking a blasphemous Argent song called "God Gave Rock & Roll To You").

This is just peachy for masses of consumers too young to know the truth. Since the remake artist is supposed to be Christian, the fans project all kinds of godly principles onto a song that has nothing to do with the Lord Jesus Christ. Here are some examples:

I JUST WANT TO CELEBRATE
- Kim Boyce

> "I just want to celebrate/ Another day of living/ I just want to celebrate/ Another day of life..."

Probably not a dozen Kim Boyce fans know it, but that song is nearly twenty years old! It was one of *Rare Earth's* all-time biggest hits. (And *Rare Earth* never even pretended to be Christians.) I can hear the kids asking now - "RARE WHO?"

There's no Jesus in this song. No Gospel. Only a generic, mindless chorus that could mean anything to anybody, anytime, anywhere. If you're looking for good, solid Bible here, it's another strikeout.

The message is exactly the opposite of Philippians 1:21-24 and 1 Peter 4:1-7.

BARGAIN – Rez Band

> "I'll pay any price just to get you/ I'll work all my life and I will/ To win you, I'd stand naked, stoned, and stabbed/ I'd call that a bargain/ The best I ever had/ The best I ever had... I'll pay any price just to win you/ Surrender my good life or bad/ To find you/ I'm gonna drown an unsung man/ I call that a bargain/ The best I ever had..."

What a POWERFUL witness for a Christ-changed life! Right? No, this song has nothing to do with salvation or the Lord Jesus! In 1971, it was a big hit for secular Rock legends *The Who*. The writer of those words is former *Who* guitarist Pete Townshend. An ex-alcoholic and infamous drug abuser, Townshend is nearly stone deaf from his years of blowing up amplifiers at the end of concerts.

But couldn't those lyrics be about Pete's search for spiritual truth, leading to conversion through the Lord Jesus Christ? Are you kidding? Townshend's "religion" has always been self-destruction and drunken, orgiastic excess. The only spiritual awakening the man ever had was an obsession with the teachings of an Eastern Sufi mystic named Meher Baba. Here's what Pete Townshend thought of his Hindu "god":

> "'Baba is Christ,' because being a Christian is
> 'just like being a Baba lover.'"[6]

So why did *Rez Band* throw out a song like
"Bargain" to their fans, if there's nothing Christian
in it? Simple: *Rez* are from a generation that grew
up on *The Who*, and *The Who* made a bundle off
this song. Why not redo it and make a bundle off
it for themselves? Who cares if it's Satan's song?
The fans will never figure it out. Most *Rez*
followers probably think *REZ* wrote it! Besides,
it's good Rock & Roll, man! Who cares about the
rest of it?

One final point about "Bargain." If a song's
LYRICS are the only real message, as C-Rock
defenders say, then how can *Rez* justify remaking
a tune with lyrics dedicated to an ANTICHRIST'S
teachings? (Sufism doesn't recognize Jesus as God
in the flesh. See 1 John 2:22,23).

SPACE TRUCKIN' - Vengeance Rising

"The fireball that we rode was moving/ But
now we've got a new machine/ Yeah, Yeah, Yeah,
Yeah the freaks said/ Man those cats can really
swing/ They got music in their solar system/
They've rocked around the Milky Way/ They
dance around with Borealice/ They're space
truckin' every day..."

If you can find something about the Lord Jesus
Christ in there, write and let me know.

As the kings of "Christian" thrash (trash), *Vengeance* have outdone themselves on this one. An 18 year-old classic by witchy Metal pioneers *Deep Purple*, this song came from a brain fried in the pits of Hell. Its lyrics were written by an Englishman named Ian Gillan, who also sang with Satan-Rockers *Black Sabbath*.

I guess *Deep Purple's* well-known drugging, fornication and occultism didn't bother *Vengeance* (especially when they paid the copyright fee to remake "Space Truckin"). Why did *Vengeance* do it? To draw deluded kids into the Heavy Metal orbit by introducing them to those "great" Rock hymns of yesteryear. These bands worship the god of Rock, so why not suck in a few thousand innocent kids (and a few tons of bucks as well)?

The name of this sneaky New Age game is deception. If there's no difference in the music, then there must be no difference in the SPIRIT either. The purpose is to merge Christ with Belial until the two are one. This is New Age synergy in action, making something new out of two opposites.

Thanks to this kind of Rock & Roll brainwashing, a whole generation of blank-eyed idolaters will be primed and ready to jump when antichrist commands. They won't know the difference between the holy and the profane. Who's to blame? Groups like *Vengeance* who are even now leading them by the nose down that fiery path to destruction.

And don't think the devil's New Age deceptions are limited to the raucous noise of the "Christian" Rock sound alone. Satan has also infiltrated music produced by the biggest and best known names in CCM. For example:

HIGHER THINGS - The Imperials

"Friend, I know where you're comin' from / Seems your life's under the gun / With no real chance of escape / There is hope right outside your door / It's what you've been searchin' for / A love that will never fade / So don't you run away / Don't run away / You can't hide / Gotta keep reachin / You must keep reachin' / Gotta keep reachin' for higher things"

Higher THINGS? What things? Your Higher Self of the New Age? The "Higher Power" of the self-help groups? While the world is busy searchin' and reachin', real Christians already HAVE the answer. His name is Jesus Christ. Why are they so afraid to just plainly say so? Maybe the Imperials should shut off their PA system for a few minutes and read Revelation 3:20:

"Behold, I (Jesus) stand at the door, and knock: if any man hear my voice, and open the door, I will come in to him, and will sup with him, and he with me."

Though *The Imperials* were at one time a good Gospel singing group, this song is a perfect example of current CCM shallowness at its generic worst (and least offensive). Sad to say, this is the mold for the majority of contemporary Christian music today. With millions of dollars on the line, the last thing these groups want to do is appear too fanatical, and thus "turn people off." Here's another case in point:

THE WONDERS OF HIS LOVE
- Philip Bailey

"The beating drums in deep forgotten forest floors/ A rhythm dance in tribal doors/ Reach the river shore/ Pounding the wonders of His love..."

Since when does God use a heathen jungle boogie to glorify His name or show His love to all mankind? The answer is simple - since Satan's New Age took control of "Christian" music!

The New Age mindset says all is one and one is all, especially in such cultural "neutralities" as music. Only a narrow minded Bible beater would be so biased as to insist pagan music is actually DEMONIC.

Bailey fails to mention that such frenzied drumfests were (and still are) used in primitive societies like the African Joujoukas to CALL UP

76

DEMONS, not exhort the greatness of Almighty God! Of course, if your god is the generic "Him" who tolerates mankind's sin no matter what, this song makes perfect sense. Thank the Lord Jesus we still have access to a Bible to set things straight:

> "And the times of this ignorance God winked at; but now commandeth all men every where to repent: Because he hath appointed a day, in the which he will judge the world in righteousness by that man whom he hath ordained; whereof he hath given assurance unto all men, in that he hath raised him from the dead."   Acts 17:30,31

CCM fans treat Philip Bailey like a saint, though he sang a duet with secular Pop star Phil Collins called "Easy Lover." Doesn't that seem strange when compared to 2 Corinthians 6:14-18?

The Bible says such unequal yoking is sin, but in the New Age it's just one more example of "unity through diversity." But that's O.K. – CCM has never cared much what the Bible says, anyway.

Philip Bailey wrote many songs about "God" during his days with his New Age/occult band *Earth, Wind & Fire*. Wicked pagan symbolism by the truckload adorned their album artwork during Bailey's membership. Here's a short list:

The all-seeing eye of Horus/Lucifer, flying saucers, pyramids galore, all manner of zodiac signs, group members dressed as priests of Babylon, the hexagram, the sphinx, the Egyptian ankh and the "4" symbol representing Jupiter, king of the gods. One of their records was even titled "I AM," a name reserved for God alone! (Exodus 3:13,14).

Here are some lyrics from an *Earth Wind & Fire* song Bailey helped write in 1975 - YEARS before he left the group and went into CCM:

SEE THE LIGHT

> "For so long, there's been such darkness/ Got to be a better way/ Keep me, Lord/ Help me to grow/ So I may reap the fruits of a free and happy soul/ Help them see the light..."

Christian catch-phrases do not make a song (or a man) a follower of the Lord Jesus Christ. And not all light is Christ's light. The very name Lucifer (god of the New Age) means "light bearing".[7] The Bible lays this out perfectly in 2 Corinthians 11:14,15:

> "And no marvel; for Satan himself is transformed into an angel of light. Therefore it is no great thing if his ministers also be transformed as the ministers of righteousness; whose end shall be according to their works."

AL GREEN

Speaking of "seeing the light," CCM star Al Green

put some interesting notes on the flip side of his 1980 album, "The Lord Will Make A Way:"

> "In these trying times, we see a bright light shining... a light that shines brighter than the noonday sun. That light is all time and space."

Those words are rank New Ageism of the first degree. Here's proof from New Age writer Dr. Rodney R. Romney:

> "So God first made light as spiritual energy and from that light created all things. We, therefore, are not made of solid, impenetrable matter - we are made of light energy. This primal force is what we call God... When people advance into the higher realms of spiritual consciousness, they often perceive this light through the spiritual sense, sometimes diffused into brilliant colors...The deep center of our inner space, where we are conscious of being filled by God, transcends all mortal limitations and brings perceptions to us that are impossible at any other level..."8

Dr. Romney's psychedelic light show sounds "really spiritual," doesn't it? As always, the Word of God lays bare such lies. Human beings aren't made of light; our origin comes from the dust of the earth! (Genesis 2:7).

Al Green's New Age allegiance doesn't stop with album liner notes. In 1989, he sang a duet with Annie Lennox, of secular Pop superstars,

Eurythmics. For those who don't know it, Lennox is a butch-headed Punk throwback who appears in concert clad in leather pants and a lacy bra. The name of her group *Eurythmics* is taken from a phase of Illuminist occultism engineered by a man named Dr. Rudolph Steiner (1861-1925).

What a coincidence that Steiner was also a member of the Order of the Golden Dawn, along with master satanist Aleister Crowley![9] The following facts about Steiner's "Eurythmics" prove the connection between the New Age and music:

> "...the Eurythmy of Steiner, and in other groups specially intoned hymns are used to awaken the necessary vibrations, setting in motion the whirling forces which attract and bring down the Master's forces from above, creating the esoteric link, concentrating the forces on the prepared focal-point..."[10]

> "[Steiner's] eurythmy appears to be magical, awakening and reawakening corresponding forces in man and in the universe, even as we know takes place in all ceremonies in these occult orders. The vibrations are set in motion by sound, rhythm, color, and movement..."[11]

> "... These movements therefore attract and bring down this same astral light, and these forces are drawn into the individual who 'becomes the bearer of the spirit self'... is this eurythmy not simply a means of creating 'vessels of light,' receivers and transmitters of these forces, hypnotically controlled by these masters, blindly

obedient to all their subtle and secret suggestions? Are they not just eurythmic mantras, potent compelling forces, awakening the Kundalini, creating illuminism, brought about by the will-power of these masters from without?"[12]

This heavy occult information can be boiled down to one simple sentence: The combination of SOUND, RHYTHM, COLOR and MOVEMENT can be used to attract demonic spirits into people. Need some hands-on experience? Watch MTV for about an hour.

Those demon spirits then brainwash and deceive humans into following their orders. This is true Illuminism, being enlightened by the power of Lucifer.

Isn't it interesting that Al Green's comments about light being all time and space match perfectly with Annie Lennox's Eurythmy? Such "coincidences" are no accident.

The song Green and Lennox resurrected was a dusty old 1960's anthem to New Age unity called "Put A Little Love In Your Heart." Their video of the tune was filled with swirling, dancing circles of light spinning through darkness. Here are the lyrics:

> "Think of your fellow man/ Lend him a helping hand/ Put a little love in your heart/ You see it's getting late/ Oh please don't hesitate/ Put a

> little love in your heart... If you want the world
> to know/ We won't let hatred grow/ Put a little
> love in your heart/ And the world will be a
> better place/ And the world will be a better
> place/ For you and me/ You just wait and see,
> people now..."

The Green/Lennox collaboration is the ultimate
in New Age "paradigm shift" (new frame of
reference). If you really want the world to be a
better place, throw a "Christian" singer and an
antichrist transvestite together. Their very presence
on the same stage proves "love" is the answer to
all our problems, and the occult eurythmy of the
light and sound drives that point into the minds
of millions.

The *Eurythmics* put out some of the witchiest
videos around, but it sure didn't bother Al Green.
Does it matter that "Put A Little Love In Your
Heart" was never intended to glorify or even
mention the Lord Jesus Christ? As long as you
have New Age "love," who needs Jesus, anyway?

The words to this song sound good until you
peer beyond the light and smoke. This kind of
deception is so slick and subtle, multitudes have
been taken in by it. Many an angry CCM fan will
argue, "It talked about love and God loves the
world, so what's the problem?" The problem is
the love they are promoting is Satan's phony
New Age love, not the true love of Jesus Christ.

82

The creed of this New Age movement and the chumps who promote it can be summed up in one sentence: Christ doesn't count, because they've found a "better way" without Him.

Here's another example of New Age propaganda in Contemporary Christian Music:

LOVE IN ANY LANGUAGE - Sandi Patti

"From Leningrad to Lexington, the farmer loves his land/ And daddies all get misty-eyed to give their daughter's hand/ Oh maybe when we realize how much there is to share/ We'll find too much in common to pretend it isn't there/ Love in any language/ Straight from the heart/ Pulls us all together/ Never apart/ And once we learn to speak it/ All the world will hear/ Love in any language/ Fluently spoken here...."

One out of five Christians reading this are surely thinking, "WOAH! Hold it right there. That song's by SANDI PATTI, and she's my favorite. She's a godly Christian, and I don't believe there's anything wrong with her! You've gone too far with this one, buddy."

If those thoughts are running through your mind, then take a deep breath and slow down. There's no doubt that Sandi Patti has produced some godly Christian music. Two stellar examples are: "I've Just Seen Jesus" (with Larnelle Harris) and the "Via Dolorosa." Here's something to consider, though:

Sandi Patti is not God. It's easy to fall into a cult of personality with CCM artists, even when their work is godly and Biblical. To put these people up on a perfection pedestal isn't fair to the artist, and it's sure not fair to Jesus. Just because a CCM star puts out some godly songs doesn't mean EVERYTHING they record matches the Word.

When we fail to closely examine ALL the music we listen to, it gives Satan a wide-open field of attack and infiltration. In the end, it's our own fault. We didn't see the devil coming, because we were too STARSTRUCK.

Sandi Patti didn't write "Love In Any Language," and that's part of the problem. (Words and music are by Jon Mohr and John Mays). In an industry as big as CCM, it's impossible for a star to personally control every aspect of their career. So what's wrong with those lyrics, anyway? Aren't they about Christ-like love for all the world?

No! The lyrics to "Love In Any Language" are as New Age as they come. The line about the Russian farmer loving his land is a slick lie. The average Russian farmer spends most of his day drinking vodka in the tractor shed. He HATES the land he works on. For more information, read the October, 1989 Reader's Digest, "Why Russia Can't Feed Itself," by David Satter, pages 62-64.

CCMers will fire back: "Alright, so they were a

little off on that first line. But what about the world seeing our love as Christians, and all nations coming together in peace as a result?"

This sounds great, but it's just not in the Bible! While Sandi sings about the coming "love" that will pull us all together, here's what the Lord Jesus Christ says is going to happen. Who's right?

> "For nation shall rise against nation, and kingdom against kingdom: and there shall be famines, and pestilences, and earthquakes, in divers places. All these are the beginning of sorrows. Then shall they deliver you up to to be afflicted, and shall kill you: and ye shall be hated of all nations for my name's sake. And then many shall be offended, and shall betray one another, and shall hate one another, And many false prophets shall rise, and deceive many. And because iniquity shall abound, the love of many shall wax cold. And except those days should be shortened, there should no flesh be saved: but for the elect's sake those days shall be shortened."
> Matthew 24:7-12, 21,22

The world's not going to turn from its wickedness by watching Christian love in action, they're going to KILL Christians instead! The kind of "love" in that Sandi Patti song is the New Age sloppy Agape, not the uncompromising "tough love" Jesus Christ exhibited everywhere He taught and preached.

The "Love In Any Language" theme is the same refried lie the *Beatles* came out with twenty years ago, "All you need is love/ Love is all you need..." It was a lie then, and it's still a lie now. What the world really needs is JESUS CHRIST. Only through Him can true Agape love for all people be a reality.

No matter how much the New Agers want it, the Bible says true peace and love won't happen until this wicked world system is totally destroyed at Christ's second coming (Rev. 19:11-21). Joey Taylor, of "Christian" Punk band *Undercover* says:

> "The bottom line... is love, not righteousness, not holiness, but love. We cannot have compassion for people if we feel we're better than they are."[13]

What Joey is really saying is, "I don't want to be constrained by living a righteous or holy life, so I'll emphasize love." But again, which love? The devil's New Age love or God's love? Obviously, it's New Age love, because God's love cannot be separated from righteousness and holiness:

> "Follow peace with all men, and HOLINESS, without which no man shall see the Lord."
> Hebrews 12:14

> "For I (Jesus) say unto you, That except your RIGHTEOUSNESS shall exceed the RIGHTEOUSNESS of the scribes and Pharisees, ye shall in no case enter into the kingdom of heaven."
> Matthew 5:20 (Emphasis author's)

The heart of the matter is this: the New Agers are doing their best to keep people fooled about their real intentions to enslave mankind. "Love" is the best smokescreen they can use to make sure this happens. New Age love is NOT the same thing as Jesus Christ's love (John 14:27).

Satan will gladly use Christian music to spread his deceptions, as long as Christians stay sleepy to the truth. "Love In Any Language" may be one of the most popular songs in churches today, but the love spoken of is antichrist's theme.

If you're thinking, "How DARE you be anti-love? " you can be assured that New Age indoctrination has already left its mark on your mind. I urge you to shake yourself and re-examine what Christ's love is really all about. It's not the sappy compromise of the New Age. The love of Jesus Christ is something much deeper:

> "This is my commandment, That ye love one another, as I have loved you. Greater love hath no man than this, that a man lay down his life for his friends. Ye are my friends, if ye do whatsoever I command you."
>
> John 15:12-14

CCM MAGAZINES

Musical mind molding is not the only avenue Satan uses in CCM today. The C-Rock magazines are full of the same cosmic garbage. Here's a prime example from an article by CCM writer John Fischer, titled "I Was Just Dreaming":

> "I'd love to see the labels fall off. I'd love to not have to call things Christian or secular anymore. I'd love for us to be creating music full of truth that shines brightly like the sun, not merely a kind of music that is only understood in a religious framework... I'd rather we weren't so trapped in dogma, so busy confirming what we already know, so eager to hear what we already agree with, that we miss another point of view that might just happen to come from God. I'd love to see Christians less concerned about getting the words right and more concerned about the heart..."[14]

Does that wonderful, uplifting bit of prose sound good to you? Watch out – it's pure New Age propaganda. And it's certainly nothing new. Another dreamer beat Mr. Fischer to the punch. Communist needle junkie John Lennon said the same thing twenty years ago! A New Ager to the core, Lennon's lyrics are the perfect mirror of CCM's current trend toward oneness, wholeness and holistic unity. For a crash course in slick deception, read the words to the most infamous New Age anthem ever produced:

IMAGINE

> "Imagine there's no countries/ It isn't hard to do/ Nothing to kill or die for/ And no religion too/ Imagine all the people/ Living life in peace... Imagine all the people/ Sharing all the world/

> You may say I'm a dreamer/ But I'm not the only
> one/ I hope someday you'll join us/ And the
> world will be as one."

The New Age says mankind can have peace without the Prince of Peace, but it will never happen (Matthew 10:34). Most CCM music embraces the same warped philosophy – love without repentance, holiness without separation, and unity at the expense of doctrine.

The New Age has manufactured a freshly painted image of born-again Christians: Divisive troublemakers standing in the face of world peace because of their refusal to be "reasonable." Satan's solution to this problem is simple – get rid of them! Thousands of years ago, Jesus Himself warned this would happen:

> "They shall put you out of the synagogues:
> yea, the time cometh that whosoever killeth
> you will think that he doeth God service.
> And these things will they do unto you,
> because they have not known the Father,
> nor me."   John 16:2,3

Worldly love will never save the world from itself. Only Jesus Christ can do that, and only true Bible-believing, born-again Christians will escape damnation when Jesus comes again (Jude 14,15 and Luke 21:25-28). By putting New Age songs at the top of the Christian Hit Parade, millions of gullible believers are even now supporting the system dedicated to their destruction.

6

What's Wrong With Copying The World?

> "If the world hate you, ye know it hated me before it hated you. If ye were of the world, the world would love his own: but because ye are not of the world, but I have chosen you out of the world, therefore the world hateth you."   John 15:18,19

Based on this scripture, it's perfectly reasonable to assume that Christians are supposed to be DIFFERENT from the rest of the world. Surely this applies to the multi-billion dollar Christian recording industry and the millions of fans supporting it.

If difference from the world is supposed to define Christian music, then the facts in this chapter present some problems.

C-Rock defenders are always saying the purpose of their music is to glorify God. Yet the quotes below prove they are more interested in being identified with the devil's crowd than anything godly. Here are a few excerpts about some of the biggest names in CCM:

KIM BOYCE

"For starters, this sounds a lot like Madonna's classy, infectious brand of dance/pop music..."[1]

RANDY STONEHILL

"I'm going back and doing a band-oriented album that stylistically is very close to the music that inspired me when I was 13 and 17 - and that's the *Byrds* and the *Rolling Stones*..."[2]

RAGE OF ANGELS

"...the Connecticut/NYC band is musically likened to *Motley Crue*, but also combines the commercially acceptable vein of *Bon Jovi*..."[3]

BARREN CROSS

"They have the sound and intensity of *Iron Maiden*."[4]

IMPERIALS

"These boys share a clear savvy of pop/rock vocal chop uncommon in this biz..."[5]

TEMPEST

"The *Poison/White Lion* fans will like this."[6]

PHILIP BAILEY

"... glides and bobs and grooves with all the style and zest you remember Philip for - in his early releases with *Earth, Wind & Fire*..."[7]

WHITE HEART

"It's everything that's right with 80's arena rock with all of the inhibitions removed."[8]

AMY GRANT

"Lyrically, the only difference between Amy Grant love songs and, say, those of Olivia Newton-John, is that often Grant's pronouns come with capital letters..."[9]

DeGARMO & KEY

"In their concerts and through their music DeGarmo & Key offer rock theology. Their uncompromising musical style has been the righteous raised fist of solid rock 'n' roll..."[10]

DANA KEY

"He describes himself as basically a blues guitarist, and it is the players from that genre that have always influenced him the most, citing B.B. King, Jimi Hendrix, and Billy Gibbons [ZZ Top] as his major mentors..."[11]

CARMAN

"Stylistically, Carman has been compared to Elvis Presley, Jim Croce, Tom Jones, Ray Stevens and even at times, Andrae Crouch. He has been described as having an Elvis-like charisma..."[12]

BOB HARTMAN *(Petra)*

"Early influences were the '70's guitar heroes like Hendrix, Clapton, Page and Walsh, and more recently Eddie Van Halen, of course..."[13]

UNDERCOVER

"... It will take Christian rock one step further with a myriad of soundscapes that combine the *Cult*, Jim Morrison, and *Alice Cooper*..."[14]

VENGEANCE RISING

"Loud, fast, heavy, thrashin' speed metal with a heavy blues influence is what you'll find on this new release from one of Christian music's most credible bands..."[15]

STRYPER

"And rock they do. Their ninety-minute stage show includes all the outward trappings of secular metal - the sass, style, and bombastic bone-jarring sonic barrage of such secular acts as *Motley Crue, Ratt, Iron Maiden*, or *Judas Priest*...."[16]

And that's just scratching the surface. I have identical quotes on the following C-Rock/CCM stars: *White Cross*, Geoff Moore, Steven Curtis Chapman, *Mad At The World*, Mark Farner, *Holy Soldier*, U2, Russ Taff, Ed DeGarmo, Phil Keaggy, *Shout*, Margaret Becker, *Petra*, Steve Taylor, Mylon LeFevre, *The Awakening, Idle Cure*, Wayne Watson, *Ruscha*, Kenny Marks, Michael Peace, Dion, Michael W. Smith, *The Choir*, Billy Sprague, Benny Hester, and Rick Cua.

WHAT DOES IT ALL MEAN?

Very simple: There is no difference between secular and "Christian" Rock music. None at all. These quotes prove that today's big CCM names learned their licks from the secular Rock & Roll monsters years ago, and are recycling that same demonic musical mess to anyone willing to listen.

The fans say, "But that's just the MUSIC. The LYRICS are where the real difference is." Alright. Let's do a little experiment. Read the following song lyrics. One is secular. One is Christian. Which is which?

BURN IN HELL

"Take a good look in your heart/ Tell me, what do you see?/ It's black and it's dark/ Now is that how you want it to be?/ It's up to you, what you do will decide your own fate/ Make your choice now, for tomorrow may be far too late/ And then you'll burn in Hell/ Oh burn in Hell/ You're gonna burn in Hell..."

SILENCE SCREAMS

"The folly in our passions/ The prisons of desire/ The foolishness of bigots/ Tinder for the fire/ In bitterness and exile/ As foolish as it seems/ In the coldest, darkest spirit/ Silence screams/ Silence screams/ The echoes roar/ Silence screams forevermore..."

Well, which one of these lyrics brings honor and glory to Jesus Christ? "Burn In Hell", with its uncompromising message of fiery judgment against sin, came from *TWISTED SISTER*, one of the most sickening groups in secular Rock! (See Figure 7[17]).

Twisted Sister Delivers A Positive Power Punch

Figure 7

Before the group broke up, former lead singer Dee Snider prided himself on his filthy mouth and transvestite appearance in pot-choked concert halls across the country. Though the message in that song was good, am I going to suggest that young people listen to a group of perverts like *Twisted Sister*? No way!

The second song, "Silence Screams" by popular C-Metal group *REZ (Resurrection Band)* was the "Christian" one. (See Figure 8[18]).

Figure 8

It's pretty sad when the heathen produce more scriptural lyrics than so-called Christian! So much for the, "It's the LYRICS that are important" argument. Try finding spiritual guidance for your life in that morbid mess *REZ* calls Christian lyrics and you'll be a long time looking.

Let's look at another set of godly lyrics:

PARTY IN HEAVEN - Daniel Band

"There's a party in Heaven/ The bread is

96

unleaven/ The tree of life is growin' fine/ It's way past eleven/ My number is seven/ The lamb and I are drinkin' new wine..."

Hmmm. Party time in Heaven, huh? Staying up past curfew and slopping down a quart or two of cheap wine with Jesus. Maybe Heaven's a swingin' place after all. Now contrast those blasphemous lyrics to the famous Satan-anthem by *AC-DC* "Highway To Hell":

"Don't need a reason/ Don't need a rhyme/ Ain't nothin' that I'd rather do/ Goin' down/ Party time/ My friends are gonna be there too/ I'm on the highway to Hell..."

The message is the same in BOTH songs. No matter where you turn up on the other side, it'll still be one big party, dude. Is it any wonder Christian youth are wallowing in ridiculous carnal compromise?

When supposedly "Christian" lyrics have the exact same message as those of the God-hating Satan-Rockers, something is drastically wrong. Even the most dedicated CCMer should be able to see the hypocrisy.What does it all prove? Simple! There is **_NO_** difference in "Christian" Rock!

BRIDE

C-Metal stars *Bride* don't even try to hide their worship of raw Satan-Rock power. At the end of their song "Heroes," ("Live To Die" album), the tortured screams of the damned wail into the blackness like the hordes of Hell let loose from the Pit.

There is also a demonic backmask hidden within those nightmarish cries. When reversed, what sounds like hundreds of whooshing, teeth-chattering voices spiral downward into a spinning mass of chaos. With shredded throats, their bellowing shrieks beg for help.[19] Please don't forget, all this is supposed to be "Christian."

"Metal Might" is a song by *Bride*. Is it about Jesus or Satan? Your guess is as good as mine:

> "The ones with the power/ They have control/ Their mere words will direct your soul/ My words of steel carry through the night/ Leaving behind the wake of Metal Might..."

Parents, if you've been wondering where all that rebellion in your kids has been coming from lately, check out this review of *Bride's* "Live To Die" album, (from a CHRISTIAN music magazine!):

> "This release is chock-full of straight-ahead, full-throttle grinding and pounding. It's the type of sound your parents will hate..."[20]

Bride outdid themselves on this next tune. How'd you like to have THESE guys play at your church next Sunday?: (See Figure 9).

Figure 9

HERE COMES THE BRIDE

"I've got the strings of fire/ Screaming guitars/
Energy that will explode/ Got the golden throat/
To put on the show/ The power I will unload/
Here comes the Bride/ Got feet of brass/ I'm
first and last..."

Jesus the guitar slinger? If this little ditty is
supposed to be about Revelation 19:11-16, *Bride*
sure missed the boat. With a Heavenly twang on

his open E power chord, Metal Messiah Jesus swoops down like a screaming jet to deliver all his hoppin' Christian headbangers from the wimpy, washed-up Devil. Shazam! The sad thing is that multitudes of young believers are buying these lies lock, stock and barrel.

A letter from aTeen Challenge worker in Salinas, California hit the C-Rock nail right on the head:

> "When my newly saved son-in-law went to a theme park on 'Christian Day' there were 'Christian groups' playing their 'Christian tunes.' The last performer rolled out on stage seated upon a throne, enveloped in smoke from a smoke machine. First he sat with a weird, sinister look, then leaping from the throne, flung himself all over the platform. After the performance Gary was so perplexed that he approached the man and said, 'Can I ask you a question? What religion do you belong to?'"[21]

Here's more musical "holiness" in action. "Master of the Metal" by the Messiah Prophet Band:

> "You hear a loud guitar/ You wonder what we are/ You say we're all the same/ You see us dressed in black/ Preparing to attack/ You say it's such a shame/ But do you really know/ The force behind our show/ Our one way ticket home/ We're rockin' for the rock/ And we will never stop/ And this you've got to know/ Jesus said upon this Rock my church will stand/... He's the Master/ The Master of the metal..."

The Rock of Matthew 16:15-18 was Peter's confession of Jesus as the Christ, NOT the Master of Heavy Metal music. That's Satan's title, as the last twenty years have proven. To answer the song's question, YES, I do know the force behind your show. I only wish every Christian teen knew. That's why this book was written.

BLOODGOOD

Most C-Rock fans refuse to believe their favorite bands are actually two-faced in what they say and do. Like gullible lambs led to a Hard-Rock slaughter, young believers eat up every golden word out of the group's mouth without a second thought. In reality, Christian young people are being taken for a BIG ride. These comments by *Bloodgood* singer Les Carlsen at a live 1987 concert are a perfect example:

> "Let's not have any of us to put down our evangelist brothers on tv. We got nothin' bad to say about 'em. Nothin'. Except that they're brothers in Christ. If they don't understand where we're comin' from, let God take care of 'em..."[22]

Match those silky words against this *Bloodgood* song to see typical C-Rock hypocrisy:

SHAKIN' IT

"He's a sinner though he'd never be found / He got caught with his own pants down / Can't

101

> imagine how he must have felt/ He should've tightened-up his Bible belt..."

Speaking of double talk, here's a letter sent to a Christian newspaper after one of our Missouri Rock music seminars. The excuses this poor, deluded girl uses are IDENTICAL to those put out by hot C-Rock fans everywhere. Remember – this young lady considers herself a Christian:

> "Who do you think you are, GOD? Well I do go to church and I do believe in God, but rock-n-roll has been around for a long time and will be around for an even longer time. No one can change that... You don't submit yourself to God, you believe in Him and know that He is there for you and in return you do the best you can and stay out of trouble... Many rock stars are self-professed witches and dabble in the occult? Who cares?... Yes, I do listen to Stevie Nicks, Prince, *Kiss, Cinderella* and *Cheap Trick*. All of these I like and I will continue to listen to. I am able because I have all of my life and will do so for the rest of it, and continue to believe in God. Why should you care who or what they believe in? Who are you to judge them or their music?..."[23]

This is how people turn out when they get their spiritual training from C-Rock stars instead of the Bible. Aren't the fruits of the Holy Spirit abounding in this young lady?: love, joy, peace, longsuffering, gentleness, goodness, faith, meekness, temperance (Galatians 5:22-23).

Why is she so angry? Because her RELIGION,

the religion of Rock & Roll, and the idols she worships were attacked.

Notice her statement, "You don't submit yourself to God." She obviously got her theology from Rock stars, not the Word of God. The Bible says we either submit ourselves to God or the devil (1 Kings 18:21.) There is no middle ground. She has made her choice, she just doesn't realize it yet.

Once young fans are programmed, Satan's mission is accomplished. CCM stars look and act like the world. Their music and lyrics are like the world. And CCM stars are promoted the same way the worldly crowd does it - through bucks and hype.

In every respect, the "Christian" music gods imitate the Hell-bound reprobates they idolized when they were younger. Is it any surprise that young CCM fans today are in worse spiritual shape than their parents? If you profess Christ, then hear what the Bible commands:

> "Love not the world, neither the things that are in the world. If any man love the world, the love of the Father is not in him. For all that is in the world, the lust of the flesh, and the lust of the eyes, and the pride of life, is not of the Father, but is of the world."
> I John 2:15-16

There's a word for the cheap, carnal counterfeits found throughout all "Christian" Rock. It's called Compromise - with a capital C.

7

What's Wrong With Christian Album Covers?

"Christian" music has fallen so far into the gutter, the artwork on CCM album covers is now WORSE than the secular stuff! The Bible minces no words about such wickedness. Here are just four the hundreds of scriptures that condemn this filth:

> "Beloved, follow not that which is evil, but that which is good. He that doeth good is of God: but he that doeth evil hath not seen God."   3 John 11

> "Her priests have violated my law, and have profaned mine holy things: they have put no difference between the holy and profane, neither have they shewed difference between the unclean and clean, and have hid their eyes from my sabbaths, and I am profaned among them."   Ezekiel 22:26

> "Let not thine heart envy sinners: but be

thou in the fear of the Lord all the day long".   Proverbs 23:17

"For to be carnally minded is death: but to be spiritually minded is life and peace."
                    Romans 8:6

As you look at the following photos, keep these scriptures in mind and don't forget – each picture is supposed to be "Christian."

PHILADELPHIA – "Search And Destroy"

Figure 10

VENGEANCE RISING – "Once Dead"

I wonder what Vengeance does with verses like:

> "This then is the message which we have
> heard of him, and declare unto you, that
> God is light, and in him is no darkness at
> all. If we say that we have fellowship with
> him, and walk in darkness, we lie, and do
> not the truth   1 John 1:5,6

REZ BAND –
"Silence
Screams"

SAINT –
"Time's End"

BRIDE – "Silence Is Madness"

8

What's Wrong With Amy, Phil, Mylon and Others?

All CCM stars claim they've found a better way to preach the Gospel and save souls. They evidently don't realize that God's way is the best way, and no man or woman on the face of the earth can ever improve on it.

The following quotes come straight from the mouth of the stars themselves. Their heart is laid bare by their words, and it's painful to see how much contempt they have for the Saviour who died for each one of them.

As you read, three alarming facts keep coming through loud and clear about their philosophy and their music:

1.) It's not based on the Bible.
2.) It's opposed to the Bible.
3.) It wants nothing to do with the Bible.

BROWN BANNISTER

Starstruck CCM fans often think their favorite idol is in complete control of the music they make, from start to finish. This just isn't true, and Amy Grant's music is probably the best example around. Brown Bannister, her long-time producer, not only sees to it that her trademark sound maintains its slick polish, he also helps write the lyrics for her tunes. Her music is a collaboration between BOTH of them. Here's how Bannister and Grant put together the "Lead Me On" album:

> "I would meet with Amy many times just talking about what the song was saying. I really enjoy producing the writing process of the song. I enjoy getting in at that level..."[1]

If you've ever wondered why Amy Grant's music has taken such a worldly turn in recent years, you have the answer. Let's see how Amy's producer looks at the lyrical content of one of the songs he helped create (about adultery):

> "....I think that might make a few people uncomfortable, that they can't face reality, that there are struggles and there is temptation. That fidelity in marriage is not an easy thing to come by, it's a very difficult thing to obtain and

110

> preserve, even as a Christian - it doesn't mean
> you still don't have red blood running through
> your veins and the same desires that everybody
> else in the world has..."[2]

"Facing reality" doesn't make me uncomfortable. But what does make me cringe is so-called Christian singers planting deadly seeds and glamorizing sins that God hates and Jesus died for (especially in so-called Christian music). The Apostle Paul, through the unction of the Holy Ghost, didn't agree with Brown Bannister. In fact, Paul said just the opposite! God tells us to FLEE fornication (1 Corinthians 6:18); not make friends with it by playing around with the idea.

Besides, I thought Christian music was supposed to bring honor and glory to Jesus Christ. Look at these lyrics to the "Lead Me On" song Bannister is referring to:

FAITHLESS HEART

> "Faithless heart/ At times the woman deep
> inside me wanders far from home/ And in my
> mind I live a life that chills me to the bone/ A
> heart, running for arms out of reach/ But who
> is the stranger my longing seeks?..."

It's not surprising that traditional Christian music gets Brown's goat as well:

> "...That's the problem I'm having with Christian

> music; it's so formula-oriented. The praise stuff
> is great, but even the praise stuff is formula. It's
> like all the same 'Okay, let's name all the names
> of God in the Bible' and 'Let's say "I will lift my
> hands"' ... I guess you just kind of run out of
> things to say when you start talking about that
> stuff. You're limited to a certain number of phrases
> that are biblical and scripturally-oriented..."[3]

In other words, let's get that old, boring, stuffy
BIBLE out of the music. We don't want that
"submission to God" and "obedience" stuff
anymore. Now we want to talk about things that
REALLY matter, things like the singer's longing
for a partner in fornication.

> "...It's very confusing because of the nature of
> religious education and upbringing and the
> separatist mentality of most churches and their
> creeds in America and their opinions on
> culture..."[4]

In these comments, Brown Bannister is saying
it's the separated, sanctified and called-out
churches who are really responsible for all this
C-Rock "bias" and intolerance. If they would just
give and bend a little, there would be no problem
accepting such worldly, whitewashed garbage.

I've got news for Brown. America's churches need
MORE separation, not less! The opposite of
separation FROM the world is mixture WITH
the world. You don't have to read very far in the
Bible to see what happened when the Israelites

112

mixed with the pagans around them. Did those pagans get saved? No way! The Israelites fell into their neighbors' sins! (See Exodus 23:28-33, Judges 2:1-3, & Leviticus 18:24-30).

Here's what Bannister thinks of the Lord Jesus:

> "...Because of anybody who's ever lived, [Jesus] is certainly the most spiritual person who ever walked the earth, in my opinion, yet he walked into bars and hung around prostitutes and tax collectors - which I guess at that time were even worse than they are now - and criminals and just all sorts of vermin..."[5]

Contrary to popular C-Rock opinion, (Bannister's own words) Jesus Christ did not "hang around" with prostitutes, criminals and vermin. To even suggest such is pure blasphemy. Jesus did move in their midst. He loved them enough to go tell them the truth; that they needed to repent and be born again. His very presence convicted those people of their sins and caused many conversions.

But Hebrews 7:26 makes it abundantly clear that Jesus Christ was SEPARATE from sinners, not part of their wicked company. Read it for yourself:

> "For such an high priest became us, who is holy, harmless, undefiled, separate from sinners, and made higher than the heavens;"

If we accepted Brown Bannister's opinion, instead

of the clear Word of God, Jesus Christ could have been found in any local brothel, laughing at the latest dirty joke, as he chugged down another bowl or two of mixed wine. What a pathetic picture these CCM spokesmen paint of our Lord! And this man is helping write Amy Grant's music.

AMY GRANT

In "DANCING WITH DEMONS", we thoroughly examined the compromise and shallowness of the "new" Amy. We discussed her condoning attitude towards drug use, premarital sex, foul language, appearing nude before men, and much more. That is enough to turn any true Christian away from this C-Rock goddess. If Jesus Christ means more to you than Amy, read these next quotes, directly from Amy. The Bible says that out of the abundance of the heart the mouth speaks (Matthew 12:34). Let's look inside Amy's heart:

> "There was a time when every song that I included on an album had a pretty spiritual content. Now I write songs about my husband or life on the farm or whatever is inspiring me at the moment..."[6]

In other words, it's more important that listeners hear about Amy's life on the farm than the Lord Jesus Christ. Yet CCM fans still insist it's the LYRICS that count? Come on.

> "I've become disillusioned, and that's why my

114

> lyrics are less idealistic. I'm realizing that the
> world isn't a perfect place, and God can't solve
> everyone's problems..."[7]

There's some great theology for young people to hear. "God can't solve everyone's problems." Young people are searching everywhere for someone to help them with their problems. They're finding that no one can. Now Amy comes along and tells them God can't help them either.

Young people who listen to real Christians will hear the truth: God can do ANYTHING! God can solve EVERY problem, no matter how big or small:

> "For with God NOTHING shall be
> impossible." Luke 1:37 (Emphasis author's).

> "If an audience feels I've walked away from
> God because I no longer talk about Him onstage,
> then that's their loss..."[8]

No, it's your loss, Amy. Someday you'll know why:

> "Whosoever therefore shall be ashamed of
> me and of my words in this adulterous and
> sinful generation; of him also shall the Son
> of man be ashamed, when he cometh in the
> glory of his Father with the holy angels.
> Mark 8:38

Here's a peek at Amy Grant's live concert "ministry":

> "That was about as close to 'testifying' as Amy got during the three-hour concert. There were no Bible verses, no worship music and no altar call. Still, there was an overall feel which can only be described as spiritual..."[9]

When a religious concert has no Bible verses, no worship music and no altar call, you have to wonder which spirit people were feeling, especially in light of the following verse:

> "Beloved, believe not every spirit, but try the spirits whether they are of God: because many false prophets are gone out into the world."   1 John 4:1

The Word of God puts the finger squarely on the spirit behind Amy Grant's concerts. Since no witnessing for Jesus Christ is done, the only spirit left is the flesh masquerading as the Holy Ghost:

> "But, beloved, remember ye the words which were spoken before of the apostles of our Lord Jesus Christ; How that they told you there should be mockers in the last time, who should walk after their own ungodly lusts. These be they who separate themselves, sensual, having not the Spirit." Jude 18,19

PHIL KEAGGY

This founder of modern "Christian" Rock shares Amy Grant's reluctance to boldly witness for the Lord Jesus:

"...Ted Nugent had come over and asked Keaggy to show him a certain lick he had played during the set. 'I said, I will if I can tell you about Jesus. Today I'd probably just teach him the lick without placing a condition on it. I was so full of zeal, so outgoing with my faith that sometimes I would push it on people. The Lord really wants us to be more giving of ourselves, and let God take care of their conversion...'"[10]

Every time these CCM kings open their mouth, it becomes more and more obvious their "religion" doesn't come from the Bible! The Lord has already stated what He expects from us, and it's not to teach pagan Rock stars guitar licks:

"But ye shall receive power, after that the Holy Ghost is come upon you: and ye shall be WITNESSES unto me both in Jerusalem, and in all Judea, and in Samaria, and unto the uttermost part of the earth." Acts 1:8 (Emphasis author's).

If people like Bannister, Amy and Keaggy aren't getting their spiritual guidance from God's Word, then where is it coming from?:

"Little children, let no man deceive you: he that doeth righteousness is righteous, even as he [Jesus] is righteous. He that committeth sin is of the devil; for the devil sinneth from the beginning. For this purpose the Son of God was manifested, that he might destroy the works of the devil." 1 John 3:7,8

117

WAYNE WATSON

CCM singing star Wayne Watson echoes Phil Keaggy's shameful compromise with these words:

> "There are three ways I can approach songwriting, and I've chosen one particular approach. There's one way I won't write. I won't write a song that says, 'You better get right with God.' From my own experience I find that way sometimes makes people defensive..."[11]

That "defensiveness" is called Holy Ghost CONVICTION, Wayne! And no one gets saved without it (John 6:44 & 16:7-11). Jesus Christ's command is the exact opposite of Wayne Watson's fence-straddling:

> "I tell you Nay: but, except ye repent, ye shall all likewise perish."   Luke 13:5

Let's be honest, Wayne. You won't lay it on the line like the Bible does because that might "offend" cash customers and cut record sales. Fellow C-Rocker Leon Patillo has already gone down that dead-end road. Here's what he found:

> "I also was trying to do crossover, and get my music out to the masses of people I thought would want to hear it. To do that we thinned out the lyric. The words were sitting on the fence. We didn't commit to the gospel side or the mainstream side. As a result, people didn't get any real meat from the music... "[12]

118

LESLIE PHILLIPS

Speaking of crossing over, here's how former CCM star Leslie Phillips (now called Sam Phillips) views her abandoned C-Rock career:

> "... I found out that the church really wasn't the place where I had more freedom, it was the opposite: I actually was restricted more. And I always felt like I was swimming upstream in that environment. I guess the main thing is, I want to grow as an artist and I want to be able to write about whatever I want to write about. And I really don't want to be restricted, and I feel like I am in Gospel music... The born-again movement is more about obsession and narrow-mindedness and repression and true Christianity is about mercy and freedom and love..."[13]

Obviously, Leslie Phillips thinks old-fashioned, born-again Christianity is some kind of horrible slavery. Was Jesus mistaken when he told Nicodemus, "Ye must be born again?" (John 3:5-8). Leslie's idea of Christianity is that sloppy old love and freedom bit, but it's nothing more than Satan's New Age philosophy in disguise.

Leslie's "I want to do what I want and not be restricted" attitude can be summed up in one word - REBELLION! It shouldn't be surprising though, since that's the hallmark of the whole CCM movement. Is Christianity really too "restrictive"? To the carnal, rebellious, fleshly mind, yes, it surely is. Romans 8:5-8 shows why:

119

> "For they that are after the flesh do mind the things of the flesh; but they that are after the Spirit, the things of the Spirit. For to be carnally minded is death: but to be spiritually minded is life and peace. Because the carnal mind is enmity against God: for it is not subject to the law of God, neither indeed can be. So then they that are in the flesh cannot please God."

Incidentally, Leslie's problem with narrow minded born-again believers would be taken care of if she would read Matthew 7:13,14. Jesus Christ was the most narrow-minded person who ever lived! (John 14:6). Match Phillips' bitter comments with these words from the beginning of her career:

> "I really believe Christian music fills a need. Whether it is meeting a person's need to understand who Jesus is or helping a person who has been a believer for a long time understand about the Lord's ways. I feel a need to be a servant in that way and reach whatever needs I see..."[14]

Why the flip-flop? Perhaps it was the Leslie Phillips concert where 1500 people walked out:

> "Many fans of contemporary Christian music were shocked when singer Leslie Phillips announced she was leaving the gospel music world to sign a recording contract with a secular record label. At a California concert in May, Phillips' new material, black miniskirt, and nonchurchy stage talk were more than many

fans could handle. An estimated 1,500 people walked out during the performance. 'I've never seen an audience react that way in my eight years of promoting,' says Robberson, who promoted the concert and formerly managed Phillips. 'Fans were disappointed and surprised, and I was in shock myself...'"[15]

Phillips' problem is shared by millions of C-Rock fans who try desperately to hold onto the world and serve Jesus at the same time. No matter how badly she or they want it, the Word of God says we should SEPARATE ourselves from worldly nonsense like Rock/Pop music and all the idolatry that goes with it. 1 Peter 1:14 tells why:

> "As obedient children, not fashioning yourselves according to the former lusts in your ignorance:"

MYLON LeFEVRE

> "I'm just a guy who's trying to teach and preach. The way I pay the rent is by playing music and selling records..."[16]

Mylon LeFevre is one of the biggest and best-known names in the CCM arena. A former drug addict and secular Pop star, Mylon kicked his habit and changed roles from Rock singer to "Christian" Rock singer in the early 1980's. An articulate and intense spokesman, he is looked on as an elder statesman for the C-Rock movement. Mylon's greatest claim to fame was his 1985 album titled "Sheep In Wolves Clothing." Its catchy title and high-octane, roaring Rock music made Mylon and his band overnight heroes for a fresh generation of boogie-bound kids.

It's sad no one bothered to tell those frothing fans that LeFevre's phrase was a twisted scripture! Matthew 7:13-23 says it's the FALSE prophets who will come as wolves in sheep's clothing, not the other way around. But then, a little bending of the Bible never hurt anyone. Isn't that right?

> "Every word of God is pure: he is a shield unto them that put their trust in him. Add thou not unto his words, lest he reprove thee, and thou be found a liar."
>
> Proverbs 30:5,6

When interviewed, LeFevre trots out the same old CCM song-and-dance about music's neutrality:

> "Music is not good or evil because of the formation of the notes or the structure of the beat. Music is good because the heart of the person playing it is innocently and sincerely giving praise to our God... During the past three years we have led almost 30,000 people into the Kingdom of God... If I could be a regular preacher and still reach kids, I would. Anyone who isn't satisfied with that answer needs to talk to Jesus about it..." [17]

Being unsatisfied with that answer, I took Mylon's advice and asked Jesus about it. Here's what the Lord said in 1 Corinthians 1:21:

> "For after that in the wisdom of God the world by wisdom knew not God, it pleased God by the foolishness of preaching to save them that believe."

Like most of his C-Rock cronies, Mylon has this scripture backwards, as this comment shows:

> "The Bible says that faith comes from hearing the Word of God, and so we sing the Word to them. Then in between songs we challenge them with the gospel..."[18]

But the Bible just said that PREACHING, not singing, is how people get saved, Mylon! There's a world of difference between music and preaching, and according to the Word, God has only ordained ONE of them to get the job done.

What about LeFevre's contention that the innocent, sincere heart of the musician makes it all o.k. in God's sight? Here's what the BIBLE says:

> "The heart is deceitful above all things, and desperately wicked: who can know it? I the Lord search the heart, I try the reins, even to give every man according to his ways, and according to the fruit of his doings."
> Jeremiah 17:9,10

Match these next two Mylon comments. Is there anything the least bit inconsistent about them?

COMMENT # 1: "We are emphasizing Jesus not

contemporary Christian music. We are not trying to convert anybody to Christian rock; we are trying to make disciples of Jesus Christ..."[19]

COMMENT # 2: "But the album we made for Epic ("Look Up") is more subtle and still has the Christian message. But it is not so religious sounding. We've been careful to avoid any religious terminology in this record that would turn people off..."[20]

There's that horrible phrase the CCMers hate so much – "turn people off." If Mylon and his buddies would read their Bibles, they'd discover that Jesus Christ "turned people off" alright. They CRUCIFIED Him for it! The Apostle Paul "turned off" some folks and ended up in a Philippian jail (Acts 16:22-25). The rest of the Apostles "turned people off" and were stabbed, clubbed and skinned alive for the Gospel's sake.

True Christians cannot help but turn some people off. When the light of real Christianity shines on the blackened heart of lost sinners, they get very uncomfortable. There's an easy way to avoid this, and CCM stars are masters at it - put out your light and wallow in the heathen's darkness with them. That's the pitted road C-Rock has chosen.

The problem with that course is no one gets genuinely converted, no one finds real peace in Christ - and very little lasting change takes place in the lives of the fans. But at least the C-Rock stars do keep raking in the bucks and basking in the fame. This self-serving mess is NOT what Christ died for.

I'M THE GREATEST

Since fat Christian resume's impress skeptics, Mylon has a whole file full of C-Rock selling points. Like grease in a pan, LeFevre loads on the butter in the following comments:

> "For me, the bottom line in this controversy over rock is a statement Jesus made: 'By their fruits you shall know them.' If you come to our concerts, you'll find people getting born again, people getting baptized in the Holy Spirit, people getting healed of physical ailments. Only God can do that, so if rock music was born in hell, somebody needs to tell God about it..."[21]

Mylon LeFevre has parroted the C-Rock party line perfectly. But he missed one very important point: *Satan's whole game is to counterfeit moves of God.* To be blinded to this is to not know your enemy (See 2 Corinthians 11:12-15). Wonder who does the blinding?:

> "But if our gospel be hid, it is hid to them that are lost: In whom the god of this world hath blinded the minds of them which believe not, lest the light of the glorious gospel of Christ, who is the image of God, should shine unto them."   2 Corinthians 4:3,4

125

Ever wonder WHY so many blinded Christians buy what Mylon LeFevre's selling without a second thought? Ephesians 2:2 has the answer - DISOBEDIENCE. (Which is plain old rebellion, the rotten root of all Rock music):

> "Wherein in time past ye walked according to the course of this world, according to the prince of the power of the air, the spirit that now worketh in the children of disobedience:"

These are just a few examples. We could go on forever. Anyone caught in the massive money-raking CCM system will either conform or be washed out. There's no place for true Bible-believing, God-honoring, soul-winning Christians in this corrupt game.

The choice is simple. Either compromise, conform and haul in the bucks, or take your narrow-minded Bible and get out. Those who choose to really serve Jesus disappear from sight. The rest keep gorging themselves on the fruits of their sin. They're the greatest, alright. The greatest hoaxsters to come down the pike in many a year.

Here's an important question only you can answer: Have they picked your pocket yet?

9

What's Wrong With Backmasking in Christian Rock?

> "For there is nothing covered, that shall not be revealed; neither hid, that shall not be known. Therefore, whatsoever ye have spoken in darkness shall be heard in the light; and that which ye have spoken in the ear in closets shall be proclaimed upon the housetops."   Luke 12:2,3

Hundreds of satanic backmasks are buried in "Christian" Rock and CCM music. Yes, you read it right. Popular CCM music contains literally HUNDREDS of subliminal messages and commands glorifying Satan/Lucifer.

I'm bringing this issue out in the open, not to glorify Satan, but to be obedient to what the Bible commands. We're not to fellowship with the unfruitful works of darkness, but rather reprove them (Ephesians 5:11).

Here is my position on backmasking, whether secular or "Christian":

Backmasking (also called metacontrasting), is not the best evidence of Satan's involvement in popular music, but it is evidence. Masses of young people are so spiritually hardened, they are not content with GOD'S TRUTH. They demand MAN'S PROOF. If you've read "Dancing With Demons" plus all the information in this book, and still see nothing wrong with "Christian" Rock, this chapter's for you. It was written for two reasons:

• To expose the true spiritual force that fuels and controls the whole CCM/C-Rock machine. His name is Satan.

• To lay one more slab of evidence on the growing mountain of negatives surrounding CCM.

What has Satan got to gain through backmasking, you ask? How about MIND CONTROL, the highest form of witchcraft. Former occultist David J. Meyer (now saved by the blood of the Lord Jesus Christ) shows how:

> "Enchantment is a form of spell casting primarily involving mind control. Enchanters dispatch or

> assign wicked spirits to objects and places for whatever purpose the spell calls for... Enchantment controls the mind and is one of the most powerful spells that can be cast on a person..."[1]

But CHRISTIANS can't have spells cast on them, can they? In the case of musical backmasks, the Christians listening cast the spell on themselves by giving a willing ear to what the devil planted in the music's subliminals (Ephesians 4:27).

Satan has a few other goals which are met quite nicely through musical backmasks:

1.) Confusion.
2.) Hardened hearts against Christ.
3.) Programmed rebellion in youth around the globe.

If you think subliminal programming is some overblown joke, why do the alcohol, tobacco and sex industries spend untold MILLIONS of dollars on it every year?

If subliminals have no effect on people, why have Belgium, Great Britain and the American National Association of Broadcasters banned their use? Why have some of the biggest Hollywood movies employed grisly "subs" in their films?

Why have major corporations like Toyota used

them in their advertising? And why have retail chains throughout America engineered massive in-store subliminal campaigns to fight shoplifting?[2]

Why? Because it works! It turns silent commands into mountains of green dollars:

> "....in 1957 people discovered a Chicago-based radio station (WAAF) had been selling subliminal advertising space at $1,000 for 400 messages aired over a four-month period...."[3]

> "Mind Communication, which reported sales of $3.5 million in 1989, is one of only a few companies in the $50 million self-help tape industry... The industry's premise is that we can recognize information presented below our threshold of awareness. Even though the listener hears only soothing music or the sound of ocean waves on an audio cassette or sees images of nature on a video, the subconscious mind can detect the hundreds or thousands of speeded-up, underlying subliminal suggestions, manufacturers say..."[4]

If there's a dollar to be made, you can bet someone will slap the label "Christian" on it and open up a whole new market. Here's the latest:

"CHRISTIAN" SUBLIMINAL TAPES

The newest buck-raker to hit the gullible Christian market is "Christian" meditation and subliminal scripture tapes. With silent commands buried deep under layers of nature sounds, these cassettes are supposed to help you learn the Word and grow in Christ. What's wrong with that? Plenty! Bible study and meditation on the Word of God is an ACTIVE process, not a passive one! Satan loves a passive mind, because it never questions; it just accepts.

This deadly nonsense is New Age mind control at its worst, and Christians are swallowing it hook, line and sinker. I wonder if the people who use this stuff have ever considered one nagging little detail:

If the subliminal instructions can't be heard, how do you know what they're telling you? Not even the companies producing this stuff will reveal THAT information:

> "Subliminal messages are undetectable by the outer mind, yet easily picked up by the inner mind which influences many of our actions, habits, abilities, likes and dislikes... You should play the tapes as often as possible but there is no need to 'consciously' listen to them. You simply turn on the tape and hear gentle ocean waves or music while you receive the desired messages without resistance from your outer mind... You can be sure that 'extra care' has gone into preparing the content. For best results, use both sides of tape at least 30 times."[5]

Don't question - just listen. That's not what the Bible says (1 Peter 5:8, 1 John 4:1, 2 Corinthians

2:11). Things get MUCH more sinister when you consider the following quote, taken from a subliminal tapes catalog:

> "The technical methods of recording the subliminal messages onto the tapes are very critical. Reproduction is successful only when using special equipment. Therefore the positive effects are lost in attempting to make duplicates from a cassette."[6]

What hogwash! Anything recorded on one cassette will be on another when copied, unless... there were SPIRIT voices on the original, put there by spells of enchantment. Too far out to believe? Satan would love for you to think so.

Speaking of spirits, a new breed of taped subliminal has hit the market. Check out these effects:

> "This tape contains no human voices. Neither does it contain any musical instruments. It is a recording of very unusual sound-wave patterns designed specifically to have profound and positive effects upon the listener..."[7]

> "According to many who have been experimenting with the... tape, they experienced physical sensations of a highly sensual and sexual nature. Some feeling such intense pleasure they could not find words to describe the feeling..."[8]

Let's get this straight. No human voices. No music.

Yet listeners go into sexual paradise whenever the tape plays. If you have had such experiences while using this stuff, you have crossed into the spirit world and are in danger of death, destruction and nightmarish attacks too awful to describe. I'm asking you in the name of Jesus Christ to repent and burn that cursed junk immediately.

SPECIAL DELIVERY

It should come as no surprise, but here's the latest – subliminal DELIVERANCE tapes! One company offers cassettes containing deliverance "subs" for 26 demonic afflictions, including homosexuality, molestation, drugs, smoking, lust, pornography and procrastination! (For a mere $698.25, you can get the whole set).[9]

Just think of it – delivered from demons without even knowing it, simply by playing one of their cassettes. No muss, no fuss. Talk about lazy spirituality. Mom's cooking supper while dad gets delivered watching the news.

That's not the way deliverance happened in the Bible. People were set free from Satan's grip through the power of God, not some stupid tape! (Mark 1:23-27) There's no doubt subliminal commands are in these things. The question is: What are they saying and why in the world would Christians give up control of their mind to voices they cannot hear? The Bible says we should be:

133

> "Casting down imaginations, and every high
> thing that exalteth itself against the
> knowledge of God, and bringing into
> captivity every thought to the obedience of
> Christ;"   2 Corinthians 10:5

Here's the real intent behind this flood of mass subliminal saturation: SATAN WANTS CONTROL OF YOUR MIND!

SUBLIMINALS IN MUSIC

So much for the self-help cassettes. What about music? The multi-billion dollar recording industry is riding the same big-buck bandwagon. Subliminal research author Wilson Bryan Key explains:

> "Subliminal technology sells records by the tens
> of millions each year in North America. No one
> apparently knows or understands as yet, however,
> the consequences of this sensory bombardment
> upon human value systems... It is not at all
> improbable that under intensive, repetitive, and
> long-term subliminal bombardment, entire value
> systems could be rearranged."[10]

If you think massive subliminal indoctrination is a joke, you should read some of the many excellent books available on this subject, such as: "Media Sexploitation," "Subliminal Seduction," and "The Clam Plate Orgy," all by Wilson Bryan Key. (CAUTION: Some of the photographs are from the sex magazine industry). Also, "The Hidden Persuaders," by Vance Packard, and "The Truth

About Backmasking," by the Peters Brothers.

Anyone who doubts Satan's power to subliminally brainwash youth through popular music hasn't been paying attention. Rock stars THEMSELVES have admitted it. Dead guitar god Jimi Hendrix revealed the conspiracy over twenty years ago:

> "Atmospheres are going to come through music, because music is in a spiritual thing of its own... you hypnotize people to where they go right back to their natural state which is pure positive... and when you get people at that weakest point, you can preach into the subconscious what we want to say..."[11]

Take careful note of Hendrix's comments. Preach into the SUBconscious what WE want to say. Who's we? Very simple: Satan and every Rock chump that ever stood on a stage. Where does this leave the stars of "Christian" Rock? - stranded in the same place as their secular buddies - deceived and deluded pawns in the devil's game of subliminal seduction through music.

Jimi Hendrix continues dropping the mask:

> "People want release any kind of way nowadays. The idea is to release in the proper form. Then they'll feel like going into another world, a clearer world. The music flows from the air; that's why I connect with a spirit, and when they come down off this natural high, they see clearer, feel different things...."[12]

There's Jimi's method of preaching - locking onto a SPIRIT of music which COMES FROM THE AIR! This is the Biblical truth of Ephesians 2:2 put into action.

BACKMASKING - HOW AND WHY?

In the summer of 1990, Rock music backmasking hit the news like a ton of bricks. Heavy Metal monsters *Judas Priest* and their record company were taken to court for allegedly contributing to the death of two fans by placing hidden messages in their music. The result was a grisly double-suicide pact that turned into a nightmare.

Two Nevada boys named James Vance and Raymond Belknap were big fans of the band. On Christmas Eve, 1985, they listened for hours to *Priest's* music, then put a shotgun to their heads and pulled the trigger. Raymond died instantly; Vance blew off most of his face, but survived for three years. The backmask in the *Judas Priest* song the boys were listening to, ("Beyond The Realms of Death") allegedly contained the following hidden message:

> **"DO IT, DO IT, DO IT, SING MY EVIL SPIRIT, F!@#$% THE LORD."**[13]

Before he finally died from his injuries in 1988, James Vance contacted a Reno lawyer:

"... after hearing what Vance had to say, [the lawyer] asked only one question: 'I said, "James, but for THAT music, would you guys have shot yourselves?" Vance said, 'No, no, no...'

" 'It was like a self-destruct that went off,' [Vance] later told a Reno journalist. 'We had been programmed...' "[14]

HOW has Rock backmasking happened? And WHY? The answer is obvious - and shocking. Satan has been using the power of the atmosphere to set the stage for antichrist since the early days of radio. When the British Broadcasting Corporation was first set up in 1923, an experimental station called 2MT was established. When the chief engineer's routine airwave test was reversed, it gave praise to Lucifer![15]

A few years later, one of the BBC's most popular radio jingles was a little ditty called "Aunt Aggie and The BBC." When the recording of this harmless slogan was reversed, a hidden message was found: "LIVE IN SIN. LUCIFER IS NICE. LUCIFER, EXPLOIT THEM!"[16]

If this sounds too far out to accept, it shouldn't. The Bible tells us in Ephesians 2:2 that there is a "prince of the power of the air," a SPIRIT that "now worketh in the children of disobedience." What is the "power of the air," if not radio, T.V. and music transmission? Go to the local shopping mall and you'll see the children of disobedience out in force - rebellious, sullen, stubborn and mad. What made them that way? The messages in popular music. If you don't think that's true, try taking their favorite music away from them for a week. You'll find yourself in the middle of World War III.

Here's where the rubber meets the road. It's not just FORWARD lyrics causing youth to spiritually rot. SUBLIMINAL indoctrination is taking place on such a massive scale, it would make our heads spin if we knew the whole truth. The "prince of the power of the air" is feverishly working to raise an army for antichrist, and backmasked messages have made his job a whole lot easier.

It's a WORLD-WIDE attack, too. Satanic backmasks in popular music have even been found in Brazil, Indonesia and Norway.[17]

But why would Satan put backmasks in "Christian" Rock? What's this wicked game of musical chairs all about? The whole purpose of C-Rock subliminals is meant to do one thing: ERASE THE DIFFERENCE BETWEEN CHRIST AND BELIAL.

Antichrist cannot be successfully received until people - especially Christians - fail to see the difference between Christ and Satan. That is the goal of "Christian" Rock backmasks - to so condition this generation that when antichrist comes, they'll fall at his feet willingly - deceived, deluded and damned.

A word of caution. We should never get so busy hunting for hidden backmasks that we overlook the ungodly FORWARD lyrics splashed throughout popular music, even "Christian" music. This song by CCM superstar Steve Taylor is a perfect example:

I MANIPULATE

"Does your soul crave centre stage?/ Have you heard about the latest rage?/ Read your Bible by lightning flash/ Get ordained by thunder crash/ Build the kingdom with a cattle prod/ Tell the masses it's a message from God/ Where the inside congregate/ I manipulate..."

Satan's two-pronged musical attack combines forward God-mocking with backmasked blasphemy. Why? To keep all the bases covered in Beast-system brainwashing. These lyrics from a Crispan St. Peter song say it all:

THE PIED PIPER

"It's your mind/ And that's all that's trickin' you/ So step in line/ Hey come on, babe/ Follow me, I'm the Pied Piper... Can't you see/ I'm the Pied Piper/ Trust in me/ I'm the Pied Piper/ And I'll show you where it's at..."

Richard Clapton's "Glory Road" is even more to

the point. It's a vivid description of Armageddon from SATAN's perspective:

> "All you children got to reap what you sow/ Self-righteous suckers... You try and take me/ I'll take you... Never surrender till that final dawn/ Never surrender till that dark cloud's gone/ I hear the thunder from the distant shore/ Some crazy general tryin to keep the score/ We took this tower here in Babylon/ Just one big flash... I'll be gone/ Here we go down the Glory Road/ Down and out/ Down and out on the Glory Road..."

Incidentally, when these lyrics are reversed, a backmask occurs, saying, "F!@# YOU, F!@# YOU, F!@# YOU..." over and over again.[18]

EFFECTS ON THE CHURCH

Well, at least the CHURCH is safe from that kind of spirit, right? You can answer that question much better than I. What kind of spirit is loose in the youth at YOUR church? Are they the children of God, or the children of disobedience?

Take a GOOD look and don't deny what your eyes tell you.

If pastors and parents allow the young people to listen to Rock and "Christian" Rock, those kids are getting the same subliminal double dose as their unsaved friends. The simple truth is this: "Christian" Rock is twice as evil as the secular stuff, because CCM appears so "holy." Dig down deep, and you'll find Satan's ugly instructions bubbling under the surface of nearly ALL Contemporary Christian Music.

But how did this happen? There are several possibilities regarding hidden messages in CCM:

1.) God is doing the "good" backmasks; Satan does the "bad" ones.

2.) The backmasks are coming directly from the singer's human spirit.

3.) Satan is secretly sabotaging true Christian artists by planting backmasks in their songs.

4.) Satan is marking his territory and at the same time subliminally programming masses of Christian youth worldwide.

Let's examine each point in detail:

"GOOD" AND "BAD" BACKMASKS

Not all CCM backmasks praise the devil. There are a handful that have supposedly "good" messages. One of the most famous examples is on Randy Stonehill's song, "Rainbow." (MESSAGE: "He shall reign forever"). Another is Dottie Rambo's "Behold The Lamb," performed by the Praise Singers. (MESSAGE: "Lamb of Glory"). Still another is found on the tune, "Greater Is He," by Dion. (MESSAGE: "His name is Jesus").

I have heard examples like these played to audiences by anti-Rock ministers. How did the crowd react? They clapped, whistled, shouted and praised God for hiding "good" messages in the music. Does God really program us subliminally to make us better Christians? According to the Word of God, no! The Bible sets this whole mess straight in Jeremiah 48:10a:

> "Cursed be he that doeth the work of the Lord deceitfully,"

John 18:20 tells us the Lord Jesus Christ never secretly manipulated anyone:

> "Jesus answered him, I spake openly to the world; I ever taught in the synagogue, and in the temple, whither the Jews always resort; and in secret have I said nothing."

The Apostle Paul didn't need hidden tricks to glorify God:

> "But have renounced the hidden things of dishonesty, not walking in craftiness, nor handling the word of God deceitfully; but, by manifestation of the truth, commending ourselves to every man's conscience in the sight of God."   2 Corinthians 4:2

These scriptures prove a powerful point. There's no such thing as "good" and "bad" backmasking. This satanic smokescreen is really a reworked version of witchcraft doctrines known as "the Force," yin/yang, and dualism. These occult laws are the base for all "white" and "black" magic. There's really no such thing as white magic, for any power apart from God comes from Satan.

Positive, "Christian" backmasking falls into the same category. Like dry water or cold heat, the communion of light and darkness is never of God (2 Corinthians 6:14). The devil is behind ALL subliminal manipulation. No matter what the message says, it's still evil. God doesn't deceive those who really want the truth:

> "And ye shall seek me, and find me, when ye shall search for me with all your heart."
> Jeremiah 29:13

And God didn't say do it backwards.

SPIRITUAL LIE DETECTORS

The second theory used to explain backmasks in popular music is called communication reversal. Simply put, the theory says this:

WHAT YOU REALLY THINK - THE REAL YOU - WILL ALWAYS BE REVEALED IF YOUR TAPE-RECORDED SPEECH IS REVERSED.

143

Applied to musical backmasking, this theory says the SINGERS are producing the messages - up from their spirits and out of their mouths. There's just one problem: You have to record and reverse their words to find out what they're really thinking. If Rock backmasks are really human spirits talking, then I'd like to hear someone explain this one:

Former *Beatle* John Lennon was shot to death in December, 1980. His "Double Fantasy" album had been in record stores for weeks. The song "Kiss, Kiss, Kiss," from that album, contains a backmask that Yoko Ono sang, which says: "WE SHOT JOHN LENNON."

If a demon didn't leave that little calling card, who did? How did Yoko Ono's human spirit KNOW, much less SAY, "We Shot John Lennon," long before the murder happened? Mark David Chapman (Lennon's killer) admitted demonic spirits gave him the strength to carry out the execution.

There's only one answer. That backmasked message on Lennon's record didn't come from a human spirit, it came from a demon's throat!

So how do these messages GET into the music? It's really very easy. The demons just talk while their Rock and CCM dupes sing. Demons are well able to speak out loud, as scripture makes abundantly clear (Mark 1:23-25 & Luke 8:28-32).

In both Australia and America, societies dedicated to communication reversal are quickly growing into grassroots industries. Full-blown seminars, media blitzes, books, tapes, videos, marketing strategies and licensed sessions to train master instructors are all part of their plan to push backward speech research around the world.

Some police departments are getting interested in the concept. If true, backwards speech applied at the jailhouse would be better than lie detectors to law enforcement. If slow-speed tape decks which also play in reverse are ever mass-marketed, look out. Everyone and their brother will be taping friends, family, and T.V. politicians to find out what they REALLY think.

Backwards speech research has tremendous potential for evil within an antichrist system. This type of pseudo-science is very appealing to the New Age mindset, since the center of attention is not God, but the human spirit of man.

It's also interesting to note the messages some UFO contactees have given during word reversal therapy. "Whirlwind" (a New Age term) appears often. Apparently, those "masters from the astral plane" like this word a lot.[19]

What a coincidence that MORIAH, the all-consuming, conquering wind, is the code name used by the Grand Druid Council of 13 for their one-world antichrist plot. Witches, wizards and the Illuminati (an elite and very satanic group of global power brokers) are all waiting anxiously for this destroying New Age whirlwind to rebuild the world THEIR way.[20] (Charles Manson called it "Helter Skelter".)

REVERSE PSYCHOLOGY?

Backwards communication in action is really the combination of a satanic principle (reversal), plus godless psychology.

The archetypes of modern psychology are all based on the teachings of Sigmund Freud and Carl Jung. Freud was a cocaine addict obsessed with sexual dysfunction. Jung was a spacy New Ager who spent most of his time somewhere on the planet Kolob.

Demonic speech manipulation in Rock backmasking is not the same thing as psychological archetype (especially since archetypes don't exist anyway). Here's an example of this kind of nonsense in action:

PSYCHOLOGY: You dreamed about running water, so you must hate your mother.

BACKWARDS SPEECH: You spoke about a

whirlwind, so you must have contacted a UFO.

MUSICAL BACKMASKING: The song reversed says "Praise the Lord," so you must be a Blood-bought Christian.

What does GOD think of forward speech with hidden messages in it?:

> "A wholesome tongue is a tree of life: but perverseness therein is a breach in the spirit."
> Proverbs 15:4

Backmasking is real, there's no doubt about that. Though they mock God and laugh at Satan, people are still hungry for an explanation. Swamped with scientific "evidence," communication reversal fills the gap. Instead of the Bible, people turn to the "experts" for answers (1 Samuel 8:6-9). Where things of the spirit are concerned, the only real experts are the Holy Ghost and the Word of God. Anything else is just wasted breath.

Proverbs 1:22,27-31 sums it all up:

> "How long ye simple ones, will ye love simplicity? and the scorners delight in their scorning, and fools hate knowledge?... When your fear cometh as desolation, and your destruction cometh as a whirlwind; when distress and anguish shall come upon you. Then shall they call upon me, but I will not answer; they shall seek me early, but they shall not find me: For that they hated

knowledge, and did not choose the fear of
the Lord: They would none of my counsel:
they despised all my reproof. Therefore shall
they eat the fruit of their own way, and be
filled with their own devices."

MUSICAL SABOTAGE?

(The Robert Skynner Affair)

If neither God nor human spirits are responsible
for C-Rock backmasking, then how does it happen?
Let's look at a third possibility. Is Satan planting
hidden backmasks in the music of godly Christian
artists to wreck their careers? Are these subliminal
messages really spiritual time bombs waiting for
some over-eager researcher to discover? The story
of an English Christian named Robert Skynner
and his experiences with Word Records should
answer that question.

Mr. Skynner sent me one of his excellent cassettes
on the subject in 1988. It was obvious he had
done his homework. His high-quality series of
Rock/Pop reversals could not be denied. The
reversed messages glorifying Satan were
overwhelming in their clarity and precision.
Particularly impressive was the solid scriptural
base used throughout the tape.

Much of Mr. Skynner's information had already
been well-established by other anti-Rock ministries
around the world. It seemed the backmasking

148

controversy had finally died down for good. Until... Robert Skynner began researching "CHRISTIAN" Rock. That's when English sparks began to fly.

During the course of his study, Brother Skynner found two obvious backmasks in songs by two of the biggest names in CCM. Both groups were under the massive Word Records business umbrella and their music was distributed in Great Britain by Word UK.

Concerned about the spiritual deadliness of satanic backmasks on Christian songs, Robert obeyed Matthew 18:15-17. He contacted Word UK's executives at their Holdom Avenue offices in Milton Keynes, England and arranged a meeting.

When confronted with the backmasking information, Word UK's sales and A&R managers denied any involvement in backmasking. Mr. Skynner's tape of reversals was sitting right on the table, but it remained unplayed. The evidence was right there. Why not listen to it?

Here is part of a statement issued by Word UK about Robert Skynner's findings:

> "....this is an issue that Word UK took up seriously when a stream of accusations were presented in a published document and an audio tape by Robert Skynner. Word entered dialogue with Mr. Skynner and invited him to their office and,

after a number of letters had passed between the two parties, he eventually visited us... As a result of this meeting Robert Skynner withdrew temporarily some accusations he had directed at Second Chapter of Acts and Petra, but we understand now has published a new brochure and is also circulating a new backward masking tape... It has always been the intention of Word to enrich the lives of consumers through exemplification, life application, and the communication of the Christian Gospel through various means..."[21]

Does one of those "various means" include backmasking? Word Records is the biggest distributor of CCM music in the world. Their powerful position as the #1 promoter of C-Rock gives them the ability to spiritually mold millions world-wide. There are several disturbing sidelights to this, and Christian writer/New Age researcher Texe Marrs shows why:

"Word, Inc., the giant Christian book and recording company, was the catalyst for this abomination [a New Age cartoon]. It was Word that first published the story book version of Kingdom Chums that ABC-TV later adapted for the tube. Moreover, ABC-TV, the conglomerate, owns Word. This is certainly sufficient proof that anything Word publishes - including all kids' materials - should be looked at carefully by Christian parents. Word's records and recordings are especially suspect: this is the company that produces an entire New Age music series, deceptively calling it 'Christian contemplative music...'"[22]

Christian author Victor Bryditzki blew the lid off the whole Word can of worms when he made the following statement:

> "If music companies like Maranatha, Myrrh, Lexicon, Light, etc. are owned and/or supported by Word, which is owned by the American Broadcasting Company, which is owned by Standard Oil, which is owned by David Rockefeller, who is owned by Philippe Rothschild, you can be sure that the church is not being illuminated by the Holy Spirit but by the Illuminati."[23]

(For more information on the Illuminati, send for a 27-page catalog by enclosing $2.75 to: Christian Truth & Victory Publications, Rt.5, Box 252-A, Alexandria, Minnesota, 56308, Tel. # (612) 846-0835.)

It's also interesting to note what an Australian backmask researcher found when he approached Word Australia in 1988:

> "They questioned me pretty thoroughly and wanted to know if I would make my findings known as he said he was concerned about sales of his albums. I told him my findings could contain negative reversals and that was the end of that!"[24]

Word UK would like C-Rock consumers to think the devil is trying to ruin godly CCM ministries by off-the-wall accusations and sneaky tricks. The whole backmasking controversy is sneered at and mocked as being too stupid for comment. Christians like Robert Skynner are then painted as wild-eyed nuts looking for demons behind every bush. The one thing completely ignored is Skynner's taped evidence. Why?

Since the artists deny using backmasks, who put those messages on there? Robert Skynner was ready to present two examples of the utmost clarity to Word UK. There ARE voices on those things! If the groups didn't do it, then there's only one answer left - Satan.

If backmasks are on "Christian" Rocker's songs (and they are), then something's drastically wrong somewhere. A doorway has been opened for satanic manipulation WITH or WITHOUT the groups' permission. By messing with Satan's MUSIC, they have left themselves wide open for all kinds of demonic devices beyond their control. One of those devices is backmasking.

And Robert Skynner's got it all on tape.

To receive more information about backmasks in popular music, as well as tracts and tapes on other subjects, write to: Robert Skynner, P.O. Box 530, London, England, E14 6AA, United Kingdom. Please remember the high cost of postage and other materials by enclosing whatever donation you can afford.

Since the first three possibilities for "Christian" Rock backmasking are all incorrect, there is only one explanation left. Satan has saturated CCM music with his evil backwards commands for one reason:

TO RAISE AN ARMY FOR ANTICHRIST

(The Michael M. Affair)

Over a two year period, Michael M. sent me 16 hours of material (ten cassettes' worth!), on backmasking in both secular and CCM music. Included were 501 individual examples, plus a 65 page synopsis on the subject.

A wide range of hidden, pro-Satan backmasked messages spanning every form of popular airwave media were exposed: cartoons, kid's shows, T.V. themes, interviews, radio ads, live church worship and TONS of secular, "Christian" Rock and CCM.

Of Michael's 500 examples, 73 have to do with Satan's mark, the mark of the devil, the evil mark, the sweet mark, the nice mark, taking the mark, worshiping the mark, counting the mark, being marked, seeing the mark, loving the mark, and getting marked for God's sake. That's more than one out of every ten messages. What's so important about this mark?

"And he [antichrist] causeth all, both small

> and great, rich and poor, free and bond, to receive a mark in their right hand, or in their foreheads: And that no man might buy or sell, save he that had the mark".
>
> Revelation 13:16,17

This has tremendous impact for masses of Rock-loving Christians. Why? Because many churches today see Revelation 13's Mark of the Beast as some hazy FUTURE event - perhaps laser tattooing or a microchip implant which will enslave the world to the antichrist economy. What most believers don't realize is: Satan is conditioning people to receive that physical mark RIGHT NOW - and he's using so-called "Christian" music to do it! But isn't that impossible? Not if you willingly open the door of your mind to the devil through Rock idolatry (Romans 6:15,16).

Here are some sobering examples from Michael M's research:

1.) The Anglo-Saxon gutter word for fornication is used often in C-Rock backmasks, especially in "Christian" Heavy Metal.

2.) Demonic voices manifest in both forward and reverse modes during LIVE church worship. In one example, a demon voice like that of a young child rails against the preaching. Other manifestations praise Lucifer in reverse even as the church worship team sings normally.

3.) Foreign language Rock songs reverse to give messages in ENGLISH.

4.) Identical words/phrases sung forward give DIFFERENT messages reversed. Yet the continuity is always the same, all-out praise to Lucifer.

This shows Satan's total control over those making the music. He doesn't need set human speech patterns to get his messages in. Once the doorway is opened, the demons say whatever they wish, regardless of the intent of the human voices.

5.) At a live "Christian" Rock concert, the words spoken from the stage have no speech reversal, but the CROWD's response DOES:

SINGER: "Hear somebody say Jesus is the Way..."

CROWD: "Hell".

SINGER: "The life..."   CROWD: "Hell".

SINGER: "Only way to get to God..." CROWD: "I'm the devil."[25]

6.) In both secular and "Christian" backmasking, the FORWARD lyrics speak to the conscious mind while the reversal hits the SUBconscious. What you hear forward is only HALF the message being given. The hidden backmask complements the forward lyric perfectly but it perverts the meaning!

The result? ONE COMPLETE SATANIC MESSAGE is dumped into the listener's soul, and they have no idea it's happening. Here's an example from a CCM song:

FORWARD LYRIC: "Raise your hands to him..."

BACKMASK: "Whose name is evil".

COMPLETE MESSAGE: "Raise your hands to him whose name is evil."[26]

THE WAY OUT

Continual repetition is the main factor behind all subliminal programming. If you truly want to remove this curse from your mind, do 2 Corinthians 6:14-18 and COME OUT of the CCM system. Stop listening to all Rock and "Christian" Rock music for the next three months and see if your thought patterns don't drastically change.

If you're not willing to do this, perhaps satanic subliminals have already completed their work on you! Only you can prove it to yourself. You'll never know how deep the devil's deception has gone in your own life until you take that first step – by COMING OUT.

THE MILLION DOLLAR QUESTION

Any C-Rock fan who's read this far is sure to

ask: "Which groups and singers are part of this? Are mine? The answer is simple. If your favorite CCM group or singer plays Pop, Rock or Funk music, they're a part! EVERY ONE! Without fail.

NO MORE EXCUSES

All this information has been laid out to rip away Satan's sneakiest mode of attack against Christian youth – subliminal messages in music. You can accept or reject what you've just read, but one thing's for sure. Any fan who still insists on listening to the ungodly noise of "Christian" Rock has no more excuse for remaining in sin.

The CCM/C-Rock system belongs to Satan. When you willingly listen to his music, you are opening yourself up to demonic subliminal attack. You have no way of knowing how much damage this tool of Lucifer has already done to you.

Christian: Please! Ask God to open your eyes so you can see how evil this whole system is. Then ask God to give you the strength you need to break free from it's grasp. The peace, joy and refreshing you'll receive as you come into total obedience and fellowship with the Lord Jesus will make it all worthwhile (John 8:32,36).

CAUTION

Be smart when listening to exposed backmasks.

Satan and his servants never intended for you to hear them consciously. Pray fervently for wisdom, protection and Holy Ghost discernment.

Use the best tools possible. Using a cheap tape deck and substandard equipment is pretty much useless. Use headphones, listen carefully, and match what you hear against the Bible. If a thrill and a chill is your main motivator, then avoid the whole backmasking issue entirely.

This information is for people who have a burden and want to know the truth. Satan has lots of traps set for spiritual thrill seekers. Don't you be one of them.

10

What's Wrong With Christian Rap?

First there was Rock.
Then came "Christian" Rock.
Then there was Rap. And now...

"CHRISTIAN" RAP

Rap "music" is the hottest thing going in churches, Christian camps and youth retreats all over the country. Teens are soaking this stuff up like sponges. They often go before the whole church on youth night to mimic routines while the latest C-Rap hit blares away in the background.

Other traveling "Christian" Rappers perform in churches, witnessing Jesus while "getting down" on those def rhymes, dude. The kids love it, of course, but most parents don't know what to think. It's all done in the name of Jesus, and to hear some tell it, C-Rap is finally bringing salvation to the streets and ghettoes of America. Can this be true? Can "Christian" Rap really lead kids to Christ? By the end of this chapter, you'll know for sure.

What is Rap "music?" Actually, it's not music at all. Rap is concentrated, electronic RHYTHM, a vibrating blast of thumping bass and droning drum machine guaranteed to rattle your brain and make your teeth grind. As the hypnotic beat pulses and thumps, the "singer" talks himself blue in the face. Every other word's a rhyme - and it's all done in perfect time.

Since secular Rap glorifies violence, murder, sexual brutality and dope/crime, the pressure is on "Christian" Rap to fill the gap. C-Rap's "positive" lyrics are pointed to as proof of its value. But C-Rap supporters are missing one vital point – there are TWO messages in any song. The lyrics are a message, AND SO IS THE MUSIC. Without the words, what exactly is Rap MUSIC saying? The answer is found in one word:

...SEX!

PREACHERS IN DISGUISE

Some people think C-Rap can keep teens away

from premarital sex. Let's see. As part of a Word, Inc. video soundtrack, a group called *Preachers In Disguise* revved up this revolting raunch-rap:

A CURRENT AFFAIR

"To bust a move was his only wish/ He was a V-E-T-E-R-A-N/ That means way back when is where he began/ She was a V-I-R-G-I-N/ He broke out after he broke her in... Sex is like wine that lightens the mind/ But done before time is like eating the rind of a lemon..."[1]

Though the crude words are supposed to be saying, "no sex until marriage", *P.I.D.'s* jivey, hip-hop, video funk-frolic gives just the OPPOSITE message to kids. The bopping crowd in front of *P.I.D.'s* big white stretch limo are in full-blown boogie abandon thanks to the sensual snakecharm of the music. The lyrics say don't do it (sort of), but the MUSIC screams out loud and clear: "SHAKE THOSE HIPS, BABY."

SAMPLING

A basic part of all Rap music is something called "sampling," pulling bits and pieces from old Rock favorites, then sewing them all together, making one big crazy-quilt of patchworked noise. Throw some hypnotic Rap chant on top of it, and you've got one class-A musical mess.

Preacher In Disguise Berry Hogan explains:

> "What people don't understand about rap, is that it brings back old music from every walk of life: R&B, country, you name it. If it was good music back in the old days, we bring it back... Rap music is like bringing to life the music of people who were dead. It's a resurrection style of music."[2]

Berry Hogan just stated one reason why "Christian" Rap should be banned from churches forever. The music that's being resurrected is from the WORLD! It's not good music from the "good old days," it's rotten and from the pits of Hell. It NEVER had anything to do with Jesus, and it represents everything that Christ is not, so why bring it back to feed the old flesh? That's not some fuddy-duddy's opinion, that's solid Bible:

> "Howbeit then, when ye knew not God, ye did service unto them which by nature are no gods. But now, after that ye have known God, or rather are known of God, how turn ye again to the weak and beggarly elements whereunto ye desire again to be in bondage?"
> Galatians 4:8,9

RAP'S ORIGIN

Where did Rap music come from, anyway? Did it begin in the ghettoes? *Preachers In Disguise* have their own explanation:

> "We're more or less real roots style, because R&B and the Blues and all that stuff came from

> the church, and so we like, we like go from like,
> like the root source and get our style... It's the
> root technique, root technique, a roots style, that's
> what we said when we was on our album... called
> it a roots style, so we got more or less a real
> roots, roots style..."[3]

I think *P.I.D.* is trying to say they've got a roots
style.

But they're dead wrong when they claim Blues
and R&B came from the Church of Jesus Christ.
That stuff can easily be traced back to the demon-
raising ceremonies of Africa, the Caribbean and
every other pagan culture.

The roots of Rap are also the roots of Rock. They
were birthed in the same place, beside the voodoo
bonfires where throbbing drums and wild dances
paid homage to the "gods" (demons):

> "Their religious worship was based on drums
> and dancing, and as they worshiped a god or
> demon, the ultimate experience was to have their
> bodies possessed by that demon. The rituals were
> grossly sensualistic and sadistic... The most
> pointed observation made in Maya Deren's book
> concerns the drummer, the rhythms and the beat...
> She observes that the dancers are forced to salute
> the drummers first before any other part of the
> ritual is entered into. It is obvious that without
> the drum, the ritual cannot progress... There is
> also no denying that the modern rock and roll
> movement evolved partially from some of the

> dances described earlier, progressing through a
> number of stages: rhumba dancing, rhythm and
> blues, rock and roll, disco, heavy metal and punk
> rock..."[4]

The evidence is overwhelming. Rap's roots are found in the hypnotic effects of nonstop drumming. The only difference is those old animal hide drumskins have been replaced by slick electronic metronomes that slap, crack and thump. The same trance-dance effects that sent people into fits of frenzy centuries ago is still going on today at Rap concerts everywhere. Why? Because Rap music came from demon worship.

"Oh," someone will argue, "'Christian' Rap is different because the words are different." No matter what the words say, the underlying message in the music is still the same: GIVE UP CONTROL OF YOUR MIND.

Toby McKeenan, of C-Rappers *DC Talk*, pulls aside the curtain:

> "Hip-hop is a different beat than R&B, it's a
> different beat than rock 'n' roll, it's a beat that
> just makes you want to dance, it makes you
> want to move... You've got to have kind of an
> attitude, it's got to be an image, so that whatever
> you're saying, you're saying it real bold..."[5]

How much plainer does it need to be? "Christian" Rap is an IMAGE. It's an ATTITUDE. Its beat makes you want to DANCE and MOVE. All those things describe what the Bible calls "the flesh." And according to the Word of God, there is no good thing in the flesh:

> "For I know that in me (that is, in my flesh,) dwelleth no good thing:"   Romans 7:18a

> "Be not deceived; God is not mocked: for whatsoever a man soweth, that shall he also reap. For he that soweth to his flesh shall of the flesh reap corruption; but he that soweth to the Spirit shall of the Spirit reap life everlasting."   Galatians 6:7,8

Those in bondage to "Christian" Rap have a hard time accepting this. Their excuse goes something like this: "The words, the words, the words. They're all that matter, and they're GOOD words. People will get saved by listening to the words!"

According to Chris Cooper, of C-Rap group *SFC*, those listening can't even understand his words!

> "The first time somebody hears it, all they're going to hear is the beat, and me rapping. But when it gets old to them, and they start hearing what I'm saying they'll begin to pick up on all the scripture I put into my music..."[6]

Chris Cooper neglects to mention one little problem: By the time they figure out the words, the music will have already done its damage to the listener's soul.

165

CHANTING FOR CHRIST?

As expected, the CCM magazines are falling all over themselves praising "Christian" Rap. Here's their definition of the movement:

> "Originally a means of communication for young people from inner-city cultures, rap music is rapidly taking American audiences by storm as a new music form that combines vocal call-and-response or solo chanting with a background of musical tracks..."[7]

Call-and-response solo chanting. Hmmm... It's interesting to match that description against a little musical history:

> "Happy music was limited almost exclusively to western civilizations, primarily because until recent years Christianity and Judaism have exercised the largest single influence on western music. Paganism, the chief influence on music in other parts of the world, has always been dominated by the dirge or chant..."[8]

Let's get this straight. Pagan music is characterized by chanting. So is Rap. But "Christian" Rap uses pagan chanting to win souls to Christ. So the end result must be: "Christian" Rappers use ungodly paganism to bring people to God! What's the Bible say?:

> "What shall we say then? Shall we continue in sin, that grace may abound? God forbid.

> How shall we, that are dead to sin, live any
> longer therein?"   Romans 6:1,2

MICHAEL PEACE

Michael Peace is one of the best-known names in "Christian" Rap. He was pulled into the Rap trap long before he got saved:

> "I had listened to rap before I was a Christian, and I liked it. I was a drummer, and I was raised on funk music. I liked anything with a good beat..."[9]

Here's how Michael approaches his preaching:

> "I know we're something now, y'all, if we have Jesus. I didn't come to tell you, you're a sinner. You can be a bunch of winners for Jesus..." [10]

Michael Peace's burden for lost youth may be sincere, but his words fly right in the Bible's face. These next verses are the very foundation of salvation:

> "As it is written, There is none righteous, no, not one: There is none that understandeth, there is none that seeketh after God. They are all gone out of the way, they are together become unprofitable; there is none that doeth good, no, not one... For all have sinned and come short of the Glory of God;"
>   Romans 3:10-12,23

Seeing their own wickedness in the Bible's mirror

is what drives people to the foot of the cross. Before accepting Christ, no one is a "winner for Jesus," but wicked lost sinners in desperate need of a Saviour. Michael Peace is painting a picture that doesn't exist in the Word of God.

THE BEAT, THE BEAT, THE BEAT

Like all CCM noise peddlers, Peace echoes the same old excuses used to defend "Christian" Rock. As long as it "relates," it must be O.K.

> "Rap is a musical form that they can appreciate - it's an interesting way to communicate with those kids... They love the sound of a strong beat and pulsating rhythm. And if they don't relate, then they don't hear the music; and if they don't hear the music, then they won't hear the message..."[11]

Here's what Peach is REALLY saying. "We are using an ungodly, sinful medium (which feeds the rotten, old flesh) to drag kids into our sin so they'll listen when we tell them they shouldn't sin. That's like shooting kids up with dope so they'll listen when they hear your anti-drug message.

The bottom line is this: kids are falling in love with Rap's gutter-grind, while the message (whatever message there is) goes right down the sewer. You don't have to be Albert Einstein to figure out one simple fact: Using sin to tell kids they should stop sinning will NEVER work!

One last word from Michael Peace:

> "I use music as a medium but I am called to be an evangelist. My call is to win souls for Jesus."[12]

If that's true, then Michael's medium should fit his message, and C-Rap doesn't even come close. The kids don't care about the words; that booming Rap BEAT buries everything around it anyway. A hypnotic, boogie-drenched sexual bump-and-grind has nothing to do with the Lord Jesus Christ.

With C-Rap saturating churches everywhere, can "Christian" prostitutes be far behind?

The original question still stands:

Will "Christian" Rap win kids to Christ? That one's easy to answer. Where in the Bible does God use hypnotism, sensuality, voodoo or electronic noise to lead souls to the Lord Jesus? The final question is the only one that really matters:

Now that you know what's wrong with "Christian" Rap, what are you going to do about it?

11

What's Wrong With
How They Look?

Hard-core C-Rockers use several different Bible twists to squirm away from their sin. One favorite is found in John 7:24:

> "Judge not according to the appearance, but judge righteous judgment."

Heads held high, they snap, "The way I look means absolutely nothing about me spiritually! The Bible doesn't say anything about the outward appearance, anyway."

Really? You don't have to read much of your Bible to see how wrong that statement is. Match the righteous Word of God against the following photos of C-Rock stars, and two obvious facts will jump out loud and clear:

1.) The outward appearance is a real key to the inner person.

2.) Wickedness cannot be hid.

WHITECROSS [1]

"O Lord, are not thine eyes upon the truth? thou hast stricken them, but they have not grieved; thou hast consumed them, but they have refused to receive correction: they have made their faces harder than a rock; they have refused to return."   Jeremiah 5:3

SAINT[2]

"An high look, and a proud heart, and the plowing
of the wicked, is sin."   Proverbs 21:4

MESSIAH PROPHET BAND [3]

"These six things doth the Lord hate: yea, seven
are an abomination unto him: A proud look, a
lying tongue, and hands that shed innocent blood,"
                              Proverbs 6:16,17

ROBERT SWEET, of *STRYPER*
"Know ye not that the unrighteous shall not inherit
the kingdom of God? Be not deceived: neither
fornicators, nor idolators, nor adulterers, nor
EFFEMINATE, nor abusers of themselves with
mankind," 1 Corinthians 6:9 (Emphasis author's).

173

HOLY SOLDIER[4]

"The lofty looks of man shall be humbled, and the haughtiness of men shall be bowed down, and the Lord alone shall be exalted in that day. For the day of the Lord of hosts shall be upon every one that is proud and lofty, and upon every one that is lifted up; and he shall be brought low:"

Isaiah 2:11,12

BLOODGOOD[5]

"The shew of their countenance doth witness against them; and they declare their sin as Sodom, they hide it not. Woe unto their soul! for they have rewarded evil unto themselves." Isaiah 3:9

BARREN CROSS[6]

"O Lord, to us belongeth confusion of face, to our kings, to our princes, and to our fathers, because we have sinned against thee."

Daniel 9:8

175

12

What's Wrong With Christian Videos?

"That's Jane Fonda in the window/ Makes me want to do some exercise/ Sing and dance/ Without an audience/ Shape those hips/ Shape those thighs/ Oooooo...Video action/ Video action..."[1]

C-Rock music has made an industry out of imitating the world. So why not copy worldly videos too? Why not capitalize on a whole segment of cash-paying Christians? The lyrics to the DeGarmo & Key song above are a perfect mirror of the shameless pandering and mindless nonsense found in "Christian" videos.

To get a quick education on the real message behind this stuff, try turning the sound OFF as you watch them. There are TWO messages in any video: 1) the music and 2) the visual action.

Arty mood shots, endless dance and concert routines, crude comedy, heavy social commentary - it's all there in the newest crop of C-Rock minifilms. Of course, there are two threads tying them all together: Rock & Roll worship - and contempt for the Church.

Curious about what exactly is going on in "Christian" videos today, I walked into a Christian bookstore recently and rented a few videos off their shelf. Here's what I saw:

RANDY STONEHILL – "Still Small Voice"

Randy is a nuclear war survivor in this one. With a blackened face and dark aviator goggles, he rolls around on a dirty mattress for the entire video while the twinkling notes of 1960's guitars push out the following message:

> "Have you heard a still small voice/ Whispering I can, I can, I can/ If you'd only believed, If you'd only believed, If you'd only believed/ That there is love..."

This chorus is repeated endlessly until someone finally shuts the camera off. "Love" will save the world? That's what the New Agers say.

AMY GRANT – "It's Not A Song"

See if you can find Jesus Christ in these deep lyrics:

177

> "It's not a song till it touches your heart/ It's
> not a song/ Till it tears you apart/ After what's
> left of what's right and what's wrong/ Till it
> gets through to you/ It's not a song..."

Amy sings this little ditty in a nursing home
where grandpas, grannies and the wheelchair-
bound patients all get hit by Amy's contagious
Pop boogie-bounce. Canes and walkers in hand,
they suddenly start break-dancing!

Go to a nursing home sometime. Do you see
anybody break-dancing there? You'll find floors
full of broken men and women who scream,
mumble and weep. "It's Not A Song" is right.
This video is a stinging mockery of age and
infirmity. No Jesus in it whatsoever.

LEON PATILLO – "Love Calling"

In this one, Leon is a hip spaceman wearing a
sparkley headband that looks like it came off a
lampshade. As he enters earth's atmosphere,
Leon's face appears on TV screens all over the
world. He begins an aerobics work-out with the
policewoman, janitor and tennis player he has
mysteriously transported to a vacant drive-in
movie lot. They begin doing the funky chicken
as Leon sings:

> "Earth people/ Please come in/ I am not alien/
> This is love calling/ Please come in/ I want to
> be your friend/ I don't want to harm you/ It's

the last thing on my mind/ I just want to share
my love with all of mankind..."

The video ends with Leon as he takes a joyride
down the highway in an open convertible. Leon
(God) is sitting in the back playing a xylophone!
As the song fades out, we hear: "Love is still the
answer to life's mysteries..."

And all this time I thought the answer was Jesus
Christ! Once again, it is obvious that CCMers
aren't interested in Jesus. They're more into
promoting Satan's New Age "love."

MYLON LEFEVRE "Sheep In Wolves' Clothing"

This video is a combination of live concert and
studio films built around the songs of Mylon
and his band, *Broken Heart*. The depth of demonic
power in this thing hits the spirit like a
sledgehammer. Mylon's lust for Rock & Roll comes
through loud and clear, from beginning to end.
It's obvious he's never given up his Rock addiction.

As the camera fades in on a concert stage awash
in multi-colored greens and reds, the crowd roars.
The drums belch out a thudding tribal beat, while
the power chords crash. Mylon, in white trenchcoat
and sunglasses, hits the groove in a guitar chorus
line. Four *Broken Hearts* are lined up on each side
of him, jerking in synch to the punch of the beat.
This is typical in all Rock concerts, as the demons

179

in the musicians crouch close to share power, before splintering off in different directions to layer spirits out over various sections of the audience. The lights come up... Let the show begin!

Broken Heart plays with the crowd like toys, stroking their spiritual ego. The music is Southern-fried boogie - wailing guitars, train-whistle leads, and a funky bass be-bop backed by drums so solid you could walk on them. PRIDE is the name of this slick game, and Mylon's show reeks of it.

MUCH is going on in the spiritual realm as *Broken Heart* takes command. LeFevre's dark glasses are being seen on more and more C-Rock faces. The demons in people prefer a darkened view of the world. Dressed in dazzling white, Mylon is the high priest who sings, "Babylon is fallen... Try to put the mark on you..."

Babylon is fallen? Not in that concert hall, it hasn't! Whether Mylon knows it or not, he's ALREADY been marked. The spirit of Babylon is all over *Broken Heart's* show. LeFevre yells at the crowd, "This is freedom... Enjoy yours! This is freedom at its best..." (See 2 Peter 2:19). The band launches into a lick-for-lick imitation of *ZZ Top* while the audience heads into feeding-frenzy.

Things break down to a blistering guitar solo storm that would make Angus Young *(AC-DC)* proud. The thousands of worshipers in that arena pay intense homage to the god of Rock - Satan, then end up singing "Amazing Grace"!

The amazing thing is this: These people bowing before Baal's Rock & Roll altar have no idea what grace is. What better blasphemy than for those principalities controlling the music and the crowd to end a guitar solo with a Gospel hymn? Can't you hear the demons shouting, "Whatta ya think of THAT, Jesus! YOUR people, screaming for ME!" The whole mess ends with a gigantic bomb flash.

Mylon's video concludes with a concept minifilm based on the song "Trains Up In The Sky." The true satanic power behind *Broken Heart* is laid bare for all to see in this one. The first thing that fills the screen is a gigantic full moon, as half-clothed natives do a wild devil-dance around a leaping campfire. A chanting drone in another language keeps time with the pounding drums while Mylon sits, his eyes hidden under black sunglasses.

The video progresses through the band's travels and ends with live concert footage. There's something very strange and disturbing about Mylon as he wails into the microphone, lights strobing all around him. He's MARKED with a double-white line across his cheek. The high priest's badge of authority.

Listen carefully and you'll hear the SAME voodoo chant behind the final chorus of "Trains Up In

The Sky" as at the beginning. Talk about the devil in action? Satan is the steam behind *Broken Heart's* power-drive. If you don't believe it, get the video and see for yourself. Absolutely chilling to anyone who has the Spirit of God within them.

While on a speaking engagement south of Chicago, my wife and I happened to turn on the T.V. one night in the motel room. At first glance, it looked like MTV, but after a few minutes, we finally figured out it was a "Christian" video station.

GEOFF MOORE & LARRY NORMAN

While C-Rockers Geoff Moore and the Distance wailed on a live concert stage, fans wild, drums pounding, guitars screaming, they kicked into a 15-year-old Larry Norman classic, "Why Should The Devil Have All The Good Music?" (Norman was a pioneer of "Jesus-Rock" in the early 70's.)

Just to give the devil his due, good old Larry ran out from the wings, his three feet of hair waving in the breeze. The band jumped around like grasshoppers on a campfire, while Larry and Geoff traded off vocals. It was the most ungodly mess I'd ever seen - all in the name of Jesus, of course. Here's what they were "singing":

> "I want the people to know/ That He saved my soul/ But I still like to listen to the radio... I ain't knocking the hymns/ Just give me a song that has a beat/ I ain't knocking the hymns/ Just

give me a song that moves my feet/ I don't like
none of these funeral marches/ I ain't dead yet..."

For someone who "ain't knocking the hymns,"
Moore/Norman sure did a great job of mocking
the Church!

"Christian" videos are the greatest brainwashing
tool to come down the pike in many a year. And
they're all saying the same thing - out with the
old - in with the new (and cool). Nowhere is this
contempt for Christian tradition more evident
than on CCM video. Here's one of the biggest:

CARMAN

"DANCING WITH DEMONS" contains one
solitary quote by Carman. Several outraged fans
have written me letters defending their CCM idol.
(Some were quite lengthy). This in itself is strong
evidence of spiritual seduction. The elevation of
any man or woman to a god-like state is plain
old idolatry. But such is the nature of all C-Rock
today, though those deceived will never admit
it. CCM has become a cult of personality because
the fans WANT it that way (See Jeremiah 5:31).

Since Carman Dominic Licciardello is such a hot
topic to multitudes of CCM fans, let's dig in and
match Carman's ministry of comedy and music
against the Bible. You might be surprised at the
results.

183

CHRISTIAN COMEDY?

Before I begin, let me say that there is nothing wrong with laughing and having a good time. But when the brunt of the jokes is my Lord and Saviour, Jesus Christ, or Bible characters like John the Baptist, the humor stops for me. John and Jesus both were executed in pain and misery. Mocking Jesus is not humor; it's pure blasphemy.

In 1988, a live Carman performance was taped at the Brady Theatre in Tulsa, Oklahoma. It was later released in cassette and video under the title, "Live...Radically Saved." The video was a huge hit all over the country, pushing Carman to new peaks of popularity.

Christian youth and adults fell all over themselves, roaring at his comic routines. They cheered and wildly applauded his dramatic readings of overblown extravaganzas like "The Champion." Was it BIBLICAL? Here's a blow-by-blow account from the video.

One of the first song routines Carman swings into is a jazzed-up 50's imitation of Elvis Presley called "Celebrating Jesus." Carman shakes, stutters and shimmies just like the "King" himself, as the crowd cheers and be-bops in the aisles. For those over 30, it's a wonderful, nostalgic trip down memory lane. Elvis admirers would surely say, "What's the big deal? That's exactly the point. It should be a VERY big deal when Christians glamorize a sex pervert, drug addict and pathetic tool of Satan like Elvis. Does this offend you? If so, then come clean and admit it: The King of Rock & Roll holds first place in your heart, not the King of Kings.

The cult of Carman shows itself during a blasphemous skit titled "Are You The One?" The packed house reacts to false Bible teaching by bursting into belly laughs! They howl at Carman's gutter-slang rendition of John the Baptist and Jesus as dim-witted cousins scratching their heads over their respective "ministries." For example:

> JOHN: "'Hey man, Hey cuz, Whatchoo doin' man? I ain't seen you in a long time. Hey, baby. How do you like my sandals, man? It's cool, alright. Do you believe, man? I'm in the MINISTRY. Do you believe this?...'

> JOHN: 'Hey cuz, Let me ask you somethin, man.'

> And Jesus turned and said, 'Hey, what's up, John?' See, Jesus is always cool; he's always together. He's got his thing together, y'know, and John said, 'Hey cuz, Let me ask you somethin. Man, you, uh, ever feel...different?'"[2]

Nose in the air, Carman does what he describes as a "Messiah-like walk," to which John replies:

> "'This is wild, brother, now I don't know. Man, I never had anybody in my family make it big. I mean, this is great...'"[3]

Jesus Christ never "made it big." But according to Carman's "comedy," Jesus hit the big time by finally figuring out he was God (a major surprise), with John the Baptist riding his coattails to fame! Is that in the Bible? You tell me:

> "He [Jesus] is despised and rejected of men; a man of sorrows, and acquainted with grief: and we hid as it were our faces from him; he was despised, and we esteemed him not. Surely he hath borne our griefs, and carried our sorrows: yet we did esteem him stricken, smitten of God, and afflicted." Isaiah 53:3,4

> "I indeed baptize you with water unto repentance: but he that cometh after me is mightier than I, whose shoes I am not worthy to bear: He shall baptize you with the Holy Ghost, and with fire:... Then cometh Jesus from Galilee to Jordan unto John, to be baptized of him. But John forbade him, saying, I have need to be baptized of thee, and comest thou to me? And Jesus answering said unto him, Suffer it to be so now: for thus it becometh us to fulfil all righteousness. Then he suffered him." Matthew 3:11,13-15

This is how Carman described the beginning of John's ministry:

> "... They grow up and they go their separate ways, and one day John comes back on the scene dressed in camel hair, eatin' bugs. You know, little locusts, grasshoppers, y'know, cockroaches..."[4] (Carman goes into a little dance step here, snickering, "La Cucarocha, La Cucarocha...")

Was John the Baptist really a drooling idiot who ate cockroaches? Here's what the BIBLE says:

> "Verily I say unto you, Among them that are born of women, there hath not risen a greater than John the Baptist: notwithstanding, he that is least in the kingdom of heaven is greater than he." Matthew 11:11

Throughout Carman's tasteless mockery, the Tulsa audience claps and yells at the top of their lungs. It's obvious that all this Bible-bashing is high class entertainment to them (as well as to thousands who bought the video). Carman continues shredding scripture:

> "Well, they go their separate ways again, and one day John gets caught and thrown in jail for preaching the Gospel of Jesus Christ, and that's where the scripture brought us. John was in jail for preaching the Gospel..."[5]

That may be good for a laugh, but it's not what the BIBLE says:

> "For Herod had laid hold on John, and bound him, and put him in prison for Herodias' sake, his brother Philip's wife. For John said unto him, it is not lawful for thee to have her. And when he would have put him to death, he feared the multitude, because they counted him as a prophet."
> Matthew 14:3-5

Carman picks up the story with John in prison.

187

Feeling sorry for himself, John paces the floor, saying:

> "... I can't die in here. No way. I ain't gonna receive that. No way. I'm a man of faith. I'm a man of power. I'm filled with the Holy Ghost... I got a big ministry. I was gonna build a big ministry. I was gonna build a big church. I was gonna name it after myself - Baptist Church." (audience roars)[6]

Was John the Baptist really a power-hungry fool who wanted a big name for himself? Why not read the REAL story. Here's what John had to say about himself and the Lord Jesus:

> "He must increase, but I must decrease."
> John 3:30

Carman finishes off his little blasphemy lesson with a snappy tune. John's disciples are seeking confirmation that Jesus is indeed the Christ. According to Carman, here's what they said:

> "You know, your crazy cousin, John the jailbird. You know, that eats bugs and stuff..."[7]

Let's get right at the root of this thing. Do you think John the Baptist would be amused at this kind of "comedy?" Would the man who was beheaded for preaching holiness and righteousness find this unscriptural garbage funny? No, he would not. But obviously thousands of Carman fans did – and do. I pray you're not one of them.

188

SUBTLE DECEPTIONS

Not every device of the devil in CCM is blatant. Young people MUST be warned about the very subtle deceptions that are being used against them by Satan. The Bible says that the serpent was more subtle than any beast of the field (Genesis 3:1). The devil will use HUMOR to drill a seed right into the listener's mind and heart. And because they're LAUGHING, they'll never give it a second thought.

Is there even such a thing as Christian comedy? Yes, of course there is. But we should NEVER laugh at Jesus or the things of the Bible. To do so is to mock the Lord that died for us, and the Father who sent Him. The next time a Christian comedian paints Jesus, John or any other Bible character as nerdy jerks, let them know that you don't appreciate them making fun of the Saviour who died on the cross for you.

The high point of the "Radically Saved" video is a masterpiece of audience manipulation called "The Champion." Moved by the music, lights and super-dramatic special effects, the crowd's emotions are played like a yo-yo in Carman's skillful hands.

The song's theme has Jesus Christ and Satan squaring off as fighters in an inter-galactic boxing ring. Surrounded by angels and demons, Jesus and the devil duke it out, one-on-one. Christ wins, of course, and the audience goes wild, jumping to their feet and hollering like a crowd of wild bulls. The problem with all this frantic, glitzy, Las Vegas-style hype is:

JESUS CHRIST AND SATAN ARE NOT EQUAL.

Read that one again:

JESUS AND THE DEVIL ARE NOT EQUAL!

It's a lie from the pit of hell to portray the Lord Jesus as the co-equal but opposite image of the devil. Satan is a created being (Ezekiel 28:13) and Jesus Christ is God (Colossians 2:8-10). When Christ shed His blood at Calvary, he spoiled principalities and powers openly, and made a spectacle of them in it (Colossians 2:15). And He did it AT THE CROSS, not in a boxing ring!

If all this is no big deal to you, then neither is the Bible. You've been had, Carman fans. Your Christianity has been turned into merchandise, and you've paid for the privilege of being fleeced.

Like most CCMers, Carman is moving away from the traditional Christian "sound." His music is getting Rockier all the time. A good example is the song "Radically Saved." On the cassette liner notes, the credits for this tune say, "Words & Music by Carman." The words may be his, but the MUSIC is a jazzed-up rehash of a moldy old secular Rock classic called "Riot In Cell Block #9" by Leiber/Stoller. (Famous 70's Blues-rocker Johnny Winter did a remake of this song on his "Saints & Sinners" album).

Here's the end result: Because their favorite star recorded a particular song, multitudes of deceived young Christians think it must be godly, holy and good. They haven't been alive long enough to know that every ten years the devil trots out his old faithful refried Rock tunes with a new coat of paint and a fresh shimmer of high-tech gloss to deceive another generation.

How can he pollute Christians with secular tunes? Simple! Have "Christian" artists perform them.

When early C-Rocker Larry Norman wrote the song, "Why Should The Devil Have All The Good Music?," he was admitting a truth multitudes of CCM fans still deny – that SATAN is the undisputed King of Rock & Roll! When CCMers step over into Satan's musical territory, whether they know it or not, they're doing Satan's business.

When Carman plays Rock, what makes HIS music immune from the devil's influence? The words may change, but the devil's MUSIC never does! Now Mr. Licciardello has even stooped to using Acid-Rock on his "Revival In The Land" album. Carman's opinion?

191

"That acid rock guitar, that real aggressive-type sound is not necessarily conducive for a lot of Christian material. There are three forms of communicating something: there's the word, the spirit, the gesture. Just because the words are there doesn't mean that you've communicated anything, because the spirit must be right, and the gesture must be right - the way the thing is presented... That type of message is conducive for that type of a sound (an aggressive, almost violent kind of sound), that type of a spirit, and that type of a performance. Therefore the song ('God's Got An Army') works."[8]

When did God start using an aggressive, violent spirit to make something "work?" But Carman is saying that as long as the song "works," it doesn't matter what kind of spirit it has. Carman won't find "the end justifies the means" in the Bible. That way of thinking is called plain old humanism.

Incidentally, Carman's "Revival In The Land" video package "works" too. It has enough occultism and demonic special effects to win an Oscar. It doesn't seem to matter that the viewer's spirit has been dragged through nine miles of bad roads by the time it's finally over.

By the way, in Christianity, I thought something "worked" when the Holy Spirit chose to bless it, with God getting all the credit. According to Carman's theology, God has nothing to do with it; MAN'S ability turned the trick. Any philosophy that shuts out the Holy Ghost is never of God.

192

If we follow that line of thinking to its logical conclusion, we'll end up exactly where the world is now - anything that "works" can't be all bad. And it all adds up to the same thing - contempt for Christ! If we can find some sure-fire formula that "works," who needs Jesus?

Since Carman claims his ministry is God-called, it would seem wise for him to stop mocking God and making Jesus Christ the butt of his jokes, while stealing all the credit for himself. Does that mean everything Carman has ever put out is rotten? Only you and the Holy Spirit can decide that. The watchword for Carman or any other CCM star can be found in 1 Thessalonians 5:21:

> "Prove all things; hold fast that which is good."

CONCLUSION

The conclusion of the matter? Most "Christian" videos have absolutely nothing to do with the Lord Jesus Christ. Big names turn slick productions into big money (and bigger reputations.) In the end, it all adds up to one thing - making merchandise out of a sneering contempt for Christ Jesus.

Do you really want to help fuel that fire with your hard-earned bucks? Think about it.

13

What's Wrong With CCM Magazines and T-Shirts?

"Only constant repetition will finally succeed in imprinting an idea on the memory of the crowd."
Adolph Hitler[1]

Satan knows if he can repeat a lie often enough, with enough sincerity and conviction, eventually millions of teens and young adults will believe it. How does the devil do it? Through CCM advertising, books and magazines.

The huge C-Rock print industry is a smoking, spinning propaganda machine that runs day and night, month after month, year after year. All the endless talk ground out through hundreds of interviews, magazines, commentaries and CCM record reviews is geared to promote one idea over and over again: "CHRISTIAN" ROCK IS THE GREATEST THING SINCE SLICED BREAD. (It also reels in mountains of money from those who suck it up like soda.) If you stacked those tons of print in one big heap, the pile would probably reach all the way to hell, because that's where it starts - in Satan's mind.

But EVERYONE is saying that "Christian" Rock is a good, valid, socially important and very spiritual way to lead millions to Christ! They can't ALL be wrong, can they? Match that slick press release against the Word of God, and you'll see that 1) Talk is cheaper than dirt, and 2) The majority has NEVER been right where God is concerned:

> "A good man out of the good treasure of his heart bringeth forth that which is good; and an evil man out of the evil treasure of his heart bringeth forth that which is evil; for of the abundance of the heart his mouth speaketh. And why call ye me, Lord, Lord, and do not the things which I say?"
> Luke 6:45,46

> "Woe unto you, when all men shall speak well of you! for so did their fathers to the false prophets." Luke 6:26

The root of all this foolishness comes down to

two points: Greed and backslidden carnality. If you don't think CCM's bedrock foundation is based on bucks, read these comments from Christian music critics who make their living off CCM compromise:

> " Sales were in a downturn, and retailers were saying, 'Hey! You guys are going to have to start putting out good music that has some substance to it...' As a result, things started to change. Lyrics became more meaningful, artists give altar calls at concerts, and with a renewed emphasis on Christ the sales slump ended. In this business, Smith says, ministry and business go hand in hand. 'You've got to sell records so you can stay in business to minister...'"[2]

That last statement is a lie straight from the pit of hell, and these guys know it! The tight-fisted greed of the C-Rock philosophy should turn the stomach of every true born-again believer. The stars didn't change their tune until the bucks started to run out! If those people really did believe in the Jesus Christ of the Bible, they'd take Him at His Word and quit worrying about their pocketbooks:

> "But my God shall supply all your need, according to his riches in glory by Christ Jesus."   Philippians 4:19

> "But seek ye first the kingdom of God, and his righteousness; And all these things shall be added unto you."   Matthew 6:33

CCM stars and fans may be looking for God's blessing, but they're running to their OWN needs first. God BLASTS and DESTROYS instead of blesses! The following quote makes this crystal clear:

> "Then there's the economic aspect of things. It's frustrating when you put five years of work into something like Allies, and are barely able to eke out a living. Contrast that with the 20 minutes Bob [Carlisle] and I spent the other day writing a country song that Dolly Parton just cut for her new album, which will probably bring in more income for us than what we make in a year with Allies..." Randy Thomas, of *Allies*[3]

If Randy Thomas would stand on Philippians 4:19, instead of trading secular tunes for quick bucks, his money problems would disappear. Matthew 6:33 means just what it says. The opposite is also true:

> "Thus saith the Lord; Cursed be the man that trusteth in man, and maketh flesh his arm, and whose heart departeth from the Lord."   Jeremiah 17:5

The following quote is the best description of the doctrine of CCM music to be found anywhere:

> "In sum: If you want to reach a broad Christian audience, minister and sell records, adopting popular secular music styles brings success. You write your own music, following the popular

> style, add Christian lyrics and send it out to the
> Christian market. That's CCM...."[4]

It sure is, and it stinks to high Heaven. No system
based on greed will ever be blessed by God:

> "No man can serve two masters: for either
> he will hate the one and love the other; or
> else he will hold to the one and despise the
> other. Ye cannot serve God and mammon"
> Matthew 6:24

"CHRISTIAN" ROCK MAGAZINES

A main source for comments like those you've
just read is a Christian fanzine called
"Contemporary Christian Music" (CCM for short).
Many imitators have sprung up in the wake of
CCM's success. Countless thousands of C-Rock
addicts treat these mags like the Bible. They don't
realize those glossy cover stories and interviews
feed the same kind of idolatry found in secular
rags like Hit Parader, Circus and Rolling Stone.

Youth! is one such magazine. Its record review
section is a favorite with Christian readers of all
ages. Music critic Bob Roth (also a chaplain at
Michigan's Albion College) writes the reviews.
Here are some excerpts:

> "Cloud nine demonstrates why George Harrison
> is still having fun. It is a work of love and
> compassion and hope and silliness. All the stuff

198

the Holy Spirit uses to give us inner power..."[5]

A few questions come to mind: Since when did the Holy Spirit start using SILLINESS to give us power in our lives? And why is this professing Christian praising the work of a pagan Hindu Rock star like George Harrison? And worse yet – what makes Roth think the Holy Spirit would use the work of an antichrist ex-*Beatle*?

Here's more pro-Rock P.R. from Bob Roth:

> "Once again, Sting is right on the mark with an album about faith, hope, and love, "... and the greatest of these is love" (1 Corinthians 13:13). Backed by an exquisite band and world-class 'extras' like Mark Knopfler and Eric Clapton, Sting sings these profound songs in his usual mellow, grainy voice."[6]

Apparently no one told Bob Roth that world-class extra Eric Clapton is one of the most infamous heroin addicts Rock music ever produced! As for Sting Sumner of the *Police*, faith, hope and love are not things he usually indulges in. Here's some of Sting's more "profound" comments:

> "I don't see the point (of being married). One can procreate without the dreaded ritual... I am terribly good in bed and I want people to know that..."[7]

Incidentally, Sting is the same guy who sang

"Murder By Numbers," a song about killing your family, or anybody else you "find a bore." Why would a supposedly Christian magazine promote perverts like Sting, when he hates everything true Christianity stands for? Because C-Rock mags can take that kind of Christian "love" all the way to the bank.

Roth outdoes himself on this next one. How would you like your Christian son or daughter heeding this man's spiritual advice?:

> "If you are into Bruce (Springsteen) worship, don't feel guilty about buying this disc. (Just admit your addiction!)..."[8]

There's some GREAT counsel to give thousands of Christian youth! "Don't feel guilty about worshiping an adulterous, God-hating Rock star and wasting your money to help support him. Just admit you're an idol worshiper and a Rock junkie, and PRESTO! everything's O.K." Sad to say, young people by the thousands are swallowing those lies.

Writers like Bob Roth have forgotten one important point, though. Not ALL young people listen to Rock music! These guys take it for granted that ALL youth (especially Christian youth) are Rock addicts. What an insult to the holy remnant of teens and young adults who are truly sold out 100% to the Lord Jesus Christ (Isaiah 1:9).

BLASPHEMY IS BIG BUSINESS

But the compromise doesn't stop there. In C-Rock advertising, blasphemy has become one BIG business. Selling Jesus Christ like a new and improved brand of dog food is the latest rage. Need proof? Take a good look through some of the CCM magazines and watch for the full-page ads promoting "Radical" T-shirts.

Christian youth supposedly order this stuff to witness Jesus to the lost. Many of these shirts sport tasteless cartoons mocking the Word of God. Never forget that blasphemy is not only CURSING the things of Christ and the Word, it's also blasphemy to make them the butt of a JOKE.

As you read the following examples, ask yourself: "Is God really glorified by cheap shots, low blows and the New Age?" You be the judge:

1.) Wearing sunglasses and shorts, white-bearded Moses sits under a parasol set between two monstrous ocean waves. Cool and serene, the old man is having a little picnic. The title of the shirt is "RED SEA BEACH CLUB." Sounds humorous until we realize this picture mocks the greatest miracle of the Old Testament, the parting of the Red Sea.

Was it a JOKE when the fleeing Israelites turned and saw Pharoah's armies thundering toward them to butcher every man, woman and child? (Exodus 14:19-31). With their backs to the water, they cried out to God to save them, and the hand of the Lord drew back the waves like parting a curtain. God saved His people and utterly destroyed the Egyptians. Is this kind of salvation and destruction supposed to be FUNNY?

2.) Or what about "SIMON PETER'S SCHOOL OF SURF"? This color-splashed shirt shows a fearless wavewalker riding the pounding surf. Another slogan in the picture says "Go boardless."

Does this mean we should snicker and sneer at the awesome account found in Matthew 14:24-32 where Peter actually walked on the water? As the wind roared, and the waves crashed, did Simon whip out his freshly waxed surfboard and call out to Jesus Christ, "Hey, dude, wanna go SURFIN'?" What stupidity. What blasphemy.

3.) Who could forget THIS classic Radical T-Shirt, titled "PARTY ANIMAL?" A Spuds MacKenzie-type dog wearing a pointed party hat is licking up a pool of vomit. The scripture beneath says, "As a dog returns to his vomit, so does the fool to his folly!"

4.) Then there's "JC/DC - JESUS CHRIST DIVINE CURRENT." This is an exact replica of the infamous *AC-DC* logo. (*AC-DC* is one of the most satanic of all the secular Heavy Metal groups).

I've got news for any Christian who thinks he's doing God a favor by wearing such an abomination in public. The copyright owners of the original *AC-DC* design don't just give it away to anyone who wants to reproduce it, not even to "Christians." Is part of YOUR money being paid to the *AC-DC* organization as a kickback to keep those shirts rolling off the line?

5.) The same goes double for "BOOK OF DANIEL OLD NO. 27" - a perfect replica of the Jack Daniels whiskey logo. (And from a distance, no one could tell the difference.) What genuine Christian would want to be identified with rotgut whiskey?

6.) If none of the above messages move you, try this one on for size: "HEAVENLY METAL - IT'LL ROCK THE HELL OUT OF YOU." If that wasn't blasphemous enough, then why not wear this T-shirt to witness Christ - The Holy Spirit dove as the BATMAN LOGO!

7.) It shouldn't be surprising that blatant New Age garbage is now part and parcel of such "Christian" slogans. Check out the following T-shirt phrases advertised in CCM magazine:

"VISUALIZE WORLD PEACE" - Visualization is an occult practice.

"WORLD PEACE THROUGH JESUS!" - Match this lie against Matthew 10:34-39.

"JESUS SAVES" - (In the form of the Coca-Cola logo!)

"GIVE PEACE A CHANCE" - This phrase was made famous in a 1969 song by Communist dopehead John Lennon. 1 Thessalonians 5:1-4 unmasks this New Age deception.

8.) If this next T-shirt slogan doesn't sicken you, nothing will: Superimposed over a giant beer label, the words say, "GODWISER – THIS BLOOD'S FOR YOU."

Speaking of tasteless, absurd advertising, CCM magazine devoted half a page of their September, 1988 issue to an ad for "JESUS THE SURFER." For a mere $18.00, readers could order a colorful poster of a Polynesian Jesus clad in a loincloth and clutching a surfboard. Ad copy read:

> "This picture, titled 'Jesus The Surfer,' is a Hawaiian portrayal of Jesus, as a hapa (multi-racial) young man, who lived by the sea as a carpenter and celebrated life by enjoying all the good things he helped create."[9]

By the way, Jesus Christ didn't "help" create anything. ALL things were created BY Him, and FOR Him, according to Colossians 1:13-19.

When outraged Christians wrote CCM magazine to complain about such rank mockery, editor John W. Styll responded like this:

"... First of all, you might wonder why a Christian magazine like CCM carries any advertising at all. There are many reasons, but frankly, the main one is economic. Advertising helps pay for the cost of publishing the magazine. Without the revenue that the ads bring in, we would have to charge about double for an annual subscription... We don't write the ad copy and there's plenty of it we could quibble with, but that's the advertiser's business - not ours.

"Despite the fact that it's OUR magazine, the space belongs to the advertiser who paid for it... We knew that running the ad for 'Jesus the Surfer' would open us up to criticism, but since we couldn't point to chapter and verse to prove it unscriptural, we let it run. Perhaps YOU can set the folks at Ho'Okumu Marketing straight. But haven't you got better things to do?"[10]

Mr. Styll would do well to read and heed Jude 17-19. The entire editorial proves two things about "Christian" Rock's big business bandwagon:

1.) If the money is on the table, anything goes.

2.) A Rock fan magazine for Christians will never make waves, just bucks.

14

What's Wrong With Promoting A One-World Church?

Today's rotten C-Rock is the logical extension of a massive spiritual counterfeit that began twenty years ago.

It started with the "Jesus Movement" of the early 1970's. This was the seedbed for the musical abominations climbing all over today's churches. The Jesus-Rock of the 70's bred the "Christian" Rock of the 80's. The story isn't over yet, but from the beginning, this whole movement was designed for one purpose:

To create the proper spiritual atmosphere to build the one-world church!

Satan knew if he could hook millions on secular Rock music, a backlash would eventually occur. When the degraded sex, dope and satanism of the 60's was trumpeted out through the Acid-Rock of the period, many said Rock & Roll had gone too far. And the question posed to the Church was - how could all those pathetic casualties of the devil's lies be reached for Jesus?

There is a basic law of Illuminism which perfectly applies here: OUT OF CHAOS COMES ORDER. (Illuminism is at the very center of the global New Age explosion. It's a religion that worships Lucifer as "the god of reason".)

In other words, create the problem, then offer the solution to the problem. The problem was a generation of lost and disillusioned hippies hungry for something real. The goal was to see them saved and born-again. Satan's marvelous answer? USE ROCK MUSIC TO WIN THEM TO CHRIST!

The devil knew that if he could entice the Church to accept and use "Christian" Rock, he would have the ultimate in ecumenism. When both Christians and the lost enjoy and defend the same musical mess, they have crossed the line of spiritual separation. They are ONE.

The destruction of all doctrinal barriers is a key building block to the antichrist's religious system. It doesn't matter that millions of Bible-believing martyrs have been strangled, burned, hung, shot and tortured for those doctrines! No, "LOVE" is all that matters in the Babylon Church. "Christian" Rock is the mortar being used to cement that new spiritual order into place. How? Part of the method comes through nostalgia:

> "It was an evening which would have been as fascinating to cultural historians as it was to these music fans. This little country church known as Calvary Chapel of Costa Mesa played a major role in providing a shelter from the storm to wayward hippies during the late '60's. Uncomplicated songs about Jesus, set to a rock 'n' roll beat, spoke to many young people trapped in the drug culture, in a way that mainline denominations never had..."[1]

The mainline denominations refused to speak the Jesus-Rock slang because they knew it for what it was - a satanic smokescreen! Here's the Jesus Movement lie in one sentence:

"Your new life in Christ is not really THAT different from your old life without Him."

I have in my files a 1973 Jesus Movement newspaper called "New Improved Truth." Its psychedelic cover is adorned with all manner of New Age imagery, including crystals, goddesses, the rainbow and an effeminate angel surrounded by lightning bolts (Luke 10:18). Other illustrations show a magic kris sword emblazoned with a hexagram, dragons and a female spirit guide leading a little boy into "higher truth." Here's an excerpt from a section titled "Faith":

> "If you've got an open channel and tune in, the Lord will fill you - your mind, your heart, your ears, your eyes! The answer's always there if you're willing to receive it, but if you resist the answer He gives, He shuts up because you won't listen. You can stick the tit in the baby's mouth, and if he takes one swig and doesn't like it, and quits swallowing, he's not going to get anymore. And mother will just give up and put him back to bed. So you have to be willing to take what he gives."[2]

After reading garbled occultic bunk like that, no wonder Christ's true Church avoided the Jesus Movement like the plague.

SALVATION - OR REBELLION?

The Jesus Movement of the 1970's was NOT street salvation designed to hit people where they lived. Instead, it was meant to create a counter-culture Church (which it did)! The long hair, marijuana haze, body stink and half-healed needle track scabs were all reasons why the newly enlightened hippies would never be welcomed in traditional churches.

Those caught up in the movement sneered at the shirt-and-tie conformists sitting behind stained glass windows. (They still do).

An important question needs to be asked. Was it the stuffed-shirt churches who wouldn't lighten up, or was it the Jesus people's REFUSAL TO CONFORM that caused the problem?

To get the answer, look around. That non-conformist spirit is still alive and well in the 1990's. Nothing has changed. A whole generation of rebels posing as Christians are still demanding, "Don't dare ask me to forsake my sinful past and conform to what the Bible says. I've got to do my own thing." Without true heartfelt repentance, every one of them will go straight into the pit of hell singing, "I Did It My Way."

Nowhere is this philosophy more evident than in music. Godly music feeds the spirit. Ungodly music feeds the flesh. Yet Jesus Movement people refuse to conform to music that truly blesses the spirit. Instead, the churches are expected to change and provide these new believers with their old flesh-feeding, foot-stomping music to keep them coming back for another dose next week. There's a word for this. It's called drug addiction.

STILL TRUE AFTER ALL THESE YEARS

Because of the Jesus Movement, one of the last strongholds of rebellion in young Christian males is still growing strong. It's found on top of their heads. If you want to get people good and mad, start preaching that men should obey God and

210

conform to what the Bible says about their hair. The spiritual sparks will fly!

Long, womanish hair on a man is a shame, according to scripture (1 Corinthians 11:14). Yet many a mop-headed Christian man refuses to cut off that shameful sign. Why? It's his symbol of REBELLION, and always will be! That was the whole reason men GREW their hair in the 60's - to rebel against all rules. The *Beatles* lit the fuse, and the spark spread like wildfire.

Rock rebellion is the root of effeminate men in our society. This country started going down when men put on lipstick, earrings and dresses. But instead of standing up against it, "Christian" Rock is full of the same stupid nonsense.

Those proud womanish locks reveal the spiritual state of the man hiding beneath them. Buzz bomb haircuts won't give you a ticket to Heaven, and having long hair doesn't send anyone to hell. It's simply a SHAMEFUL thing, according to the Bible.

IDOLATRY is the real problem here. Those wild, moon-teased mousse-dos are the most blatant symbol of rebellion in Christian youth and the gods they worship - the CCM/C-Rock stars. Many of the big names in C-Rock today are holdovers from the rebellious 60's. THAT'S why they still flaunt their hair like women. They never gave up their rebellion OR their idol-worship.

Hit this issue, and you'll see some C-Rockers scream with anger! "That doesn't matter," they'll yell. "Jesus doesn't care how I look!"

Yes, my friend, he does. Jesus Christ will take you just as you are. No one can clean themselves up enough to come to Christ (Romans 3:10-23). But if you're truly born-again and submitted to God's authority, there will be a difference in the way you walk, the way you talk, the way you look, and even the way you smell! (2 Corinthians 5:17).

Simply put, the Jesus movement was a PRODUCT of a rebellious society, not the answer to society's problems. Many well-meaning, sincere converts to Christ were devoted to what they thought was a godly thing.

But the movement itself was designed by Satan to sow rebellious seeds. Twenty years later, the haughty lives and attitudes of too many Christian youth prove it.

LARRY NORMAN

The story of C-Rock pioneer Larry Norman is a perfect case in point. Larry and his guitar-twanging buddies thought "Christian" Rock music was based on Jesus, but REBELLION was its real root. Read this excerpt from a 1989 C-Rock newspaper:

"The time was the early 70's, the Jesus Movement was in full swing, and music was what mattered. Problem was, most all of it was being made by artists that wouldn't be caught dead in a church. Hope arrived in the form of the holy trinity: Mylon, Love Song and Larry Norman... Larry Norman was just what the doctor ordered for most of us. He was the closest thing to a bona fide rock star that we could find; sporting long, straight white hair that could offend our parents, Norman wrote like Dylan and sang like Jagger, and created an almost mythical mystique about himself that really worked. Larry Norman mattered..."[3]

MUSIC was what mattered. LARRY NORMAN, god-king of "Christian" Rock - mattered. Not Jesus Christ. Offending parents and worshiping at the Rock & Roll altar was the real name of the game. If that's not rebellion, what is?

Refusal to conform IS rebellion. The Jesus hippies and their offspring today are still holding onto that devil's lie. With teeth gritted and both feet dug deep in the ground, they demand the Church change to please them. Their philosophy is - "To conform is death. I'd rather die."

MUSIC'S NEW PURPOSE

Through the Jesus Movement, Satan built a counter-culture Church from the ground up, laying the foundation for the C-Rock of today. Satan's plan has worked amazingly well. Just as the

POLITICAL changes in 1990's Europe are molding one-world government, the SOCIAL changes (brought about through music) are building one-world religion.

Someone who doesn't think Rock music changed global morals, habits and spirituality has either been hiding in a foxhole for 35 years, or was born yesterday. Look around - Rock influence is all over fashion, print, video, philosophy, amusement, education and... the Church.

The method to this madness? To mold masses of people into one vast herd - in politics AND religion. Unity at ANY cost is the plan, and "Christian" Rock is a major tool to make it all come together. If you need proof, it's as close as the secular music world.

WHY are Rock giants like Paul McCartney and Sting Sumner of the *Police* suddenly throwing all their weight behind saving the ecology and feeding the hungry? They didn't care much about those things while they were raking in their millions. (McCartney even admitted he was a COMMUNIST during his *Beatle* years!)[4]

The masters that pull the strings of these Rock puppets have given them a brand-new agenda. No more of that dope and sex stuff. Now it's time to save the planet before it's too late. If a few billion people have to give up their rights, be eliminated, or driven from their homes in the process... well, that's the way it goes.

THE MASTER PLAN

Incidentally, Illuminism, New Ageism, Nazism, Communism and Humanism are all the same thing. There really is nothing new under the sun, for all of these "isms" were part of Nimrod's Tower of Babel society - and God crushed it (Genesis 10:8-10 & 11:1-9). In a nutshell, the Illuminati scheme calls for three things:

1. **Destroy America as a sovereign nation.**

2. **Create a new computer currency through world-wide Depression.**

3. **Abolish Christianity.**

These goals can be accomplished by exploiting the wretched Third World to make gullible Christians think GLOBALLY, and act LOCALLY. It's "unity through diversity," and the CCM dupes are at the forefront of the movement. Rock stars, both secular and "Christian," are up to their necks in these concepts, and the end of the road leads to one person – Antichrist.

Woodstock, "We Are The World" and Live Aid were all stepping-stones for this plan. Now the CCMers have initiated phase two!

By imitating their secular cousins, the big CCM names back the same one-world themes through their own pet projects like: Compassion International, World Vision, Agape, AIDS Crisis and Christian Today, Christian Artists United To Save The Earth, and Carry the Light.

Here's a partial listing of CCM supporters: Steve Camp, Sheila Walsh, Sandi Patti, Randy Stonehill, Phil Keaggy, Bill Gaither, Margaret Becker, *Petra*, Leslie Phillips, *Bash 'n the Code*, and *The Choir*.

In 1988, over twenty CCM stars appeared in "SHAKE - Christian Artists Face The Music." Participants included: Mylon LeFevre, Philip Bailey, Russ Taff, Steve Taylor, Greg X. Volz, David Meece and Benny Hester.

SHAKE was a massive public relations campaign by Word/Myrrh Records to hit church youth groups with slick CCM star interviews and snatches of throbbing Rock & Roll in a hip radio format. Copies were sent free as promo materials to prove how sincere these artists really were.

Its purpose was to build the bedrock foundation from which antichrist will draw his followers. Those CCM stars are the new prophets and priests for a Rock-saturated generation of Christians. Satan's not about to let a pool of souls like that slip through his grasp. When those CCM gods and goddesses mount their soapbox, masses of fans will be right there waiting. Where Rock daddy leads, the C-Rock kids blindly follow. Satan has duped his children well, and he did it by addicting them to Rock & Roll.

CCM supporters have a valid question: "What's wrong with feeding the hungry and saving the earth?" Nothing, as long as it fulfills GOD's plan, not the Illuminati's.

The Lord made clear at the Tower of Babel that anything leading to one-world government was NOT His will. People can be fed, clothed and evangelized without jumping onto some superstar-studded bandwagon full of media glitz and magazine hype.

The Bible plainly states we will always have the poor with us (Matthew 26:11, John 12:8). Poverty and want will never be totally erased in this present world. The scriptures also state that mankind will NEVER be able to save the earth from being destroyed (Matthew 24:21,22). This old world is doomed for destruction, and the death blow will come from God's own hand! (Isaiah 24:1-7,19,20).

Where do the fans fit into all this? They're the wild card in the Illuminist plan, because people-control is the name of the game. Led by the Holy Spirit's discernment, true Christians will have nothing to do with such sneakiness. Real Christians know the end of the age is upon us, and they know the Bible says deception will be a hallmark of the end (Matthew 24:4,5,11,24).

Yet masses of devoted CCM lovers will fight to the death defending their right to Rock. Since Rock & Roll brainwashing makes gods out of men and women, the fans who follow those gods refuse to believe they could be tricked, used or manipulated by a system that has done so much "good."

This is true satanic deception in action: getting Christians to worship the very Beast system that is preparing to kill them!

CCM music is the spiritual key Satan will use to unlock the one-world Church and let loose the lions.

15

What's Wrong With Christian Thrash?

Someone is sure to ask, "What in the world is "Christian" Thrash?" Here's the definition: Punk-Rock and Heavy Metal combined - all in the name of Jesus, of course.

Here are just a few sweet titles from some popular C-Thrash bands: *Torn Flesh, Choose Death, Dancing Naked, Cut The Crap, Love Kills* and *Infected.* Check out this lovely, scriptural song by a C-Thrash group called "Persecution":

> "Praise The Lord - Beat My Head In."

Persecution also has some uplifting, godly lyrics in their music that are sure to lead lost kids to Christ. Here are two examples:

"Drown the Devil in the urinal."

"I love my dog, and he loves me/ He uses my leg when he has to pee..."[1]

ONE BAD PIG

Singer Paul Q-Pek of the C-Thrash band *One Bad Pig* is a man with a mission. Paul and his group are part of a devoted ministry team. This is what they talk about when they get together:

> "We've placed ourselves under a couple of authorities in our church. They're cool guys. They understand what we're doing and come up with an objective viewpoint... All of us are men, we talk about subjects that are open. One topic we talk about is masturbation. They minister to us so that we're equipped to minister with other people who come to us... We're definitely not rock stars. I have to come home and use the bathroom like everyone else..."[2]

Paul isn't bashful when it comes to sharing his philosophy:

> "If our music or name or dress is offensive to people, that's fine. Christ offended a lot of people."[3]

There are two big differences, Paul. 1) You're not Jesus Christ. 2) Jesus offended people because He told them the truth. You offend people because you're disgusting.

GET YOUR HEAD SPLIT FOR JESUS

There is a phenomenon that goes on at "Christian" Thrash concerts called "Moshing for the Master." Kids run along the lip of the stage and dive head-first into the crowd below, while masses of Thrashers slam into each other like slaughterhouse steers waiting for the butcher. They call these places "mosh pits." How good it must feel to know you've just been hit in the face for Jesus.

One of the biggest developers and supporters of new "Christian" Thrash groups is an organization called "Sanctuary." (Their logo is punctuated by a sacrificial knife.) Writer David Koen, in the Phoenix, Arizona newspaper *New Times*, defines Sanctuary this way:

> "... Sanctuary, a four-year-old church chain in southern California, has lured more than 350 followers of rock and the Rock. Headed up by a towering presence these Christians gushingly call Pastor Bob, Sanctuary reels in cleaned and uncleaned fish with an 800 number that dishes out info on bands and Bible..."[4]

With a three-foot mass of curly perm draping his shoulders, Sanctuary head honcho Bob Beeman is primary spokesman for the movement. Here's Bob's description of Moshing:

> "It's 'ring-around-the-rosey' heavy metal style. It's basically skipping with your arms up."[5]

So moshing is like school kids skipping through a field of daisies on a warm summer day? Does Bob Beeman really expect us to believe that snow job? This letter from a 15-year-old Chicago girl tells the real story:

> "... I see absolutely nothing Christian about diving into an audience on top of people or running around like maniacs, risking being trampled to death! This kind of violence has no place in a Christian concert. No violence at all should be involved!..."[6]

Amen. Sometimes it takes children to teach adults common sense.

EXCUSES, EXCUSES, EXCUSES

Listen to some of the limp-wristed excuses C-Thrashers use to justify their violent concerts:

> "If something occurs in a Christian audience, then something will be done about it..." Roger Martinez, of *Vengeance Rising*[7]

Gee, that's comforting, Roger. Sounds like Mr. Martinez would NEVER encourage an audience to become violent, doesn't it? A 1987 Sanctuary video called "Metal Mardi Gras" proves otherwise.

In this live concert film, Martinez "does something" all right. Eyes rolling like marbles, he twitches and falls about the stage while the other band members whipcrack their heads in furious, jerky circles. The pounding, triple-time funeral dirge of the music perfectly matches his guttural, choking grunts. In the midst of the churning chaos his music has just ignited, Martinez stokes up the crowd like a bellowing cheerleader:

"THIS IS OUR LAST SONG TONIGHT. YOU BETTER THRASH! YOU BETTER THRASH ON THIS ONE, MAN. IT'S THE LAST SONG FOR TONIGHT. IF YOU WANNA GET GOIN', YOU'D BETTER DO IT NOW..."[8]

The drums take off like a piston-slapping steam boiler ready to blow. The crowd responds by accelerating into a contorted sea of spastic madness. You can see spirits hit those kids like sledgehammers, making them jerk, twist and scream. Those children are in the grips of enough demonic power to crush them like twigs. And the band played on...

Is anyone really naive enough to think those frothing, headbanging, wild-eyed fans were dancing in the Holy Spirit? The demon let loose at that concert has a name - Abaddon the Destroyer! (Revelation 9:11):

NEUTRAL BEATS DON'T BEAT UP KIDS

Here's how CCM magazine described the Sanctuary show:

> "Deliverance and Vengeance, the two debut acts on Beeman's newly formed Bottomline Records, dished out a meaty helping of genuine thrash metal, which got the first eight rows to bang their heads to the furiously fast beat..."[9]

Hey! Wait a minute. I thought the beat was supposed to be neutral. As harmless as a Lawrence Welk waltz - isn't that what Bob Beeman and his buddies say? How convenient. And what a lie. The powers behind "Christian" Thrash are selling a slick, slippery bill of goods to gullible believers and church leaders everywhere. Don't fall for it!

When the kids go wild, these C-Thrash bands whine like babies. They refuse to admit it's their MUSIC that throws those fans into demonic fits:

> "What good is it to have a Christian band that plays speed metal if they [the audience] are gonna be violent? But then again, how are we gonna reach the violent kids that are into speed metal if we don't play it?" Glen Rodgers, of *Deliverance*[10]

Rodgers' philosophy says this: "We'll wallow in the pigsty with them so we can tell them their sin is wrong." There's just one little problem. After a while, the hogwallow gets full, and EVERYBODY'S covered with muck. Who's clean enough to preach then, Glen?

If the "Christian" Thrash leaders REALLY wanted to help some young people, they'd read and heed their BIBLE. God's Word says to clean up your own act first by separating from the world's filth, THEN take the Gospel to others (Matthew 7:1-6).

If these people tried a little PREACHING under the anointing of the Holy Ghost, (1 Corinthians 1:21) they might see the violence replaced by tears of repentance. That's how people really get saved, not by making noise that slam-bashes kids into each other like mindless ping-pong balls.

DELIVERANCE FROM EVIL

On April 7, 1989, my wife, my pastor and I saw *Deliverance* "play" to a crowd of young headbangers in Bedford, Indiana. I went so I could speak from personal experience. And what an experience it was.

There were no seats; everyone stood or sat on the floor. Once *Deliverance* hit the stage, their "music" threw the fans into instant fits of demonic devil-dance. When the drummer poured on the gas, a young man next to us leaped off the ground, his arms flinging right and left while his head jerked back like he'd been hit with a tire jack. Lost in the jet-engine roar, his body convulsed and twitched in spastic seizures. His eyes were tightly shut. We dove into a corner to keep from being slugged by his swinging fists. Others were doing the same thing all over the room.

225

Our hearts broke for one little 11-year-old girl. Parked directly in front of the P.A. stacks, her body trembled like she was being electrocuted. Her eyes glazed over while the band's noise pushed the upper limits of the human pain threshold. What hope have kids like that got? Force-fed a diet of demonic slop in the name of Jesus, and some mother somewhere thinking it was all "Christian."

When it came time for the "preaching," the members of *Deliverance* took turns talking about love and victory and not being a "wimp." Nothing about repentance. Nothing about salvation or separation from the world. Instead of an altar call, there was a cattle-call yodel where all the Christians were instructed to yell for Jesus.

If you want to see abomination in action, check out one of these "Christian" concerts. It will turn your stomach (at least it should).

Unfortunately, the biggest print resource for the Contemporary Christian Music movement (CCM magazine) sees nothing wrong with any of this. Shredding the scriptures is fine as long as people get what they want. Writer Doug Van Pelt says:

> "Thrash metal, like other contemporary forms of Christian music, may be one of those rare occasions where the 'means' ARE justified by the 'ends'."[11]

See if this makes sense to you: Junior or daughter comes home from the "Christian" concert with blood all over their face. "Hey Mom, guess what! I had a great time getting my nose broken for Jesus! And everybody got saved!"

STRAIGHT FROM THE HORSE'S MOUTH

As time goes on, it's getting harder and harder for these C-Rockers to hide the real purpose of their "music" - REBELLION! The following interview with Bob Beeman is a good case in point. It was conducted by pro-"Christian" Rock ministers Dave Hart and Al Menconi. (Hart works at Menconi Ministries, and also leads a Sanctuary "church" in San Diego.)

> DAVE HART: "... Is it okay to sacrifice traditional church standards to win kids to Christ? I think God says yes."[12]

Where does God say that, Dave? In 1 Timothy 4:1? Or is it in 2 Timothy 4:3,4? Maybe it's in Titus 1:9-11.

> DAVE HART: "Is it okay to compromise moral and spiritual principles to win kids? The answer is obviously no. Biblically, the ends do not justify the means. Where the church gets into trouble is when it assumes that God follows the church's standards and traditions. Appearance, volume, style, and culture are not spiritual standards. They are man-made standards. We can't

227

invalidate a fruitful ministry just because its methods don't meet with church tradition."[13]

Let's take this statement one point at a time:

1.) "Biblically, the ends do _not_ justify the means."

But Doug Van Pelt and CCM magazine just said they DID! (Incidentally, CCM editor John W. Styll sits on the Advisory Board of Trustees at Al Menconi Ministries.)

2.) "Where the church gets into trouble is when it assumes that God follows the church's standards..."

Hart has it backwards. God doesn't follow the church's standards and traditions, WE FOLLOW GOD'S. And it's God's standards, not the Church's, that prove "Christian" Thrash to be ungodly, rotten, and wicked.

3.) "Appearance, volume, style, and culture are not spiritual standards."

See chapter 17 if that's your excuse.

4.) "We can't invalidate a fruitful ministry..."
Dave Hart may not want to, but God already did! When is a "fruitful" ministry invalidated? When the fruits are ROTTEN; when they don't match the Word of God.

It's time for some solid Bible, instead of cheap psychology and Aristotelian logic. Here's what the Bible says about "Christian" Rock, Pop, Thrash and all the other trash that goes with it:

Galatians 5:19-21 lists 17 works of the flesh, and Romans 7:18 makes it clear there is no good thing in the flesh at all. Let's take a look at some of the sights you'll see at "Christian" Rock concerts. How do they match up with Galatians 5?:

1. Leather, Chains and Studs:
   • Uncleanness, sado-masochism & bondage

2. Womanish hair on men:
   • Shameful and unnatural (1 Cor.11:14)

3. Moshing for the Master:
   • Violence and the spirit of murder

4. Harlotry in the women:
   • Fornication and adultery

5. Party-time atmosphere:
   • Lasciviousness, revellings

6. "Preaching the Gospel" through an ungodly medium:
   • Heresies

7. T-shirt slogans, jewelry and group identification in the fans:
   • Idolatry (See Isaiah 3:16-24)

The Menconi/Beeman interview continues with a discussion about the "Christian" Thrash group *Vengeance*. In February, 1990, *Vengeance* released an album called "Once Dead." The band members were pictured on the cover as livid corpses crawling up out of their graves. The songs inside contain such sweet titles as "Cut Into Pieces" and "Frontal Lobotomy" (A lobotomy is an operation where part of the brain is surgically removed).

VENGEANCE
"Human Sacrifice"

AL MENCONI: "What about Vengeance? They are the most extreme thrash/speed metal ever put out in a Christian setting. The vocals sound like demons. They sound angry and rebellious. Isn't this music a worldly compromise? How can these guys really be honoring the Lord?"

BOB BEEMAN: "I put Vengeance together myself. I hand-picked the people to infiltrate the underground thrash-metal scene. Personally, I hate the music.

"My hand is pictured on the Vengeance album cover; I sing back-up on the album; I helped produce the album... I'm very pleased with the members of the band. Roger Martinez, the lead singer, is the pastor of the Sanctuary church in Hollywood. You honestly won't find many men that are as grounded in the Word, that know their Scripture like he does. You also won't find anyone who's a better exhorter than Roger Martin, the guitarist. He's one of the elders at the church in Redondo Beach. So is Glenn Mancaruso, the drummer..."[14]

230

Sounds wonderful, Bob, but you didn't answer any of the questions. Of course, if I was you, I'd probably sidestep questions like those too. Let's see what kind of gospel kids who buy this tape are getting. Check these Vengeance lyrics:

BEHEADED

"I want (my) head chopped off/ You'll see (my) body rot/ But then (I'll) reign with Christ/ And then you will fry..." (This song ends with tortured human screams).

BOB BEEMAN: "That's why we started Sanctuary in the first place. How do we decide if this is really of God or not? How do we decide if this is a valid ministry? The Bible says you look at the fruit and see what it's producing..."[15]

Exactly! Moshing, shallow, ungodly, unscriptural, confused young people is the fruit of this kind of "ministry." There's no better example than Sanctuary's own C-Rock video used to promote their movement.

"Metal Mardi Gras 1987" features an interview with two teenage girls dressed straight out of Isaiah 3:18-23. When asked why they've come to see the Sanctuary concert, one replies that her CHURCH is sponsoring the event! The other says she just "loves Heavy Metal."

Here's how *Vengeance* "spread the Gospel" as they

played to the headbanging crowd lurching in front of the stage:

> "*Vengeance* played the shortest song of the night, 'Receive Him,' which started with a quick drumroll, followed by about two seconds' worth of rapid-fire basic rock chords and the words 'Receive Him!' That was all..."[16]

Receive who? Jesus Christ or Satan?

C-Metal superstars *Bloodgood* also made an appearance at the concert. Here's how they glorified Jesus Christ during their set:

> "During the song 'Crucify,' singer Les Carlsen came out dressed as Pilate, deliberating Jesus' fate. Later in the song the band depicted the flogging of Jesus, as bassist Michael Bloodgood and guitarist David Zaffiro took turns whipping and kicking Les, creating a stunning portrayal of Jesus' suffering..."[17]

Stunning.

The high point of the Sanctuary video comes when a purple-haired punk in sunglasses takes the stage, holding a massive Bible. Is he there to minister the Word of God to the assembled crowd of kids? Not according to this quote:

> "I'm not here to tell you about how much Jesus loves you because you already should know that. He does love you, but that's not what I'm here

to talk about. I'm here to talk about me!..."[18]

With an absurd fake English accent, this nut proceeds to give a discourse on the Ten Commandments. Mr. Purple Punk's interpretation of the Fourth Commandment about keeping the Sabbath day holy is full of deep meaning:

"That means, like, veg out on Saturdays..."[19]

With spiritual leadership like this, who needs antichrist?

The 1970's Jesus Movement was the dry run for 1990's abominations. Yet fans of "Christian" Rock and C-Thrash still refuse to face up.

If you profess Christ as your personal Saviour, you should read and study the next two chapters. If the Word of God means anything to you at all, I pray the scriptures that follow will speak to your heart and reveal the truth to your soul – that "Christian" Thrash is an abomination in the sight of Almighty God.

16

What's Wrong With My Excuses?

Every excuse in the book, no matter how ridiculous, has been given to show why C-Rock MUST be used to minister to youth and young adults. Let's look at ten of the most popular excuses and match them against the Bible. You be the judge. If the excuse matches the Word, then accept it. If not...

1.) They're going to listen to Rock music anyway! At least this is a better alternative.

The first part of that statement is a bold-faced lie. Not every new convert is as hard-hearted and rebellious as the CCM stars. Many young people are giving their hearts and lives completely to the Lord at salvation and have turned away from vile Rock filth. I've got a file drawer full of their precious letters. They recognize the difference between the holy and the profane, and are choosing holiness.

But what about the "better alternative?" Are you kidding? C-Rock looks the same, sounds the same and produces the same rotten fruit as its secular cousin: rebellion. It teaches kids how to love the New Age and hate authority. Some alternative.

2.) We have to use C-Rock because this is the music kids relate to today.

2 Corinthians 6:14-18 tells Christians to SEPARATE from every ungodly work, not invite it home for dinner!

Here's the heart of the problem - the "relating" hoax is really about friendship WITH sin, not coming out from among them and being separate. Instead of "touch NOT the unclean thing", C-Rock says: "Touch it all you want to! We'll use it as a bridge to get to something better! Who cares if God forbids it? What does He know, anyway?"

Another point to consider: If you as a pastor, parent, youth leader, or church have to use gimmicks like "Christian" Rock to "relate" to youth, where does this leave the ministry of the Holy Ghost? Matthew 7:6 says not to throw pearls before swine. Yet we've got it backwards! We'll dump Rock filth in the laps of God's people and call it a blessing!

A "Christian" Thrash singer once told me I'd probably get my teeth knocked out if I went into the ghetto to witness. He said I'd have no chance of getting anyone to listen to the Gospel looking like that. (I was dressed in a shirt and tie.)

This man didn't know that two nights before, I was dressed the same way and shared the Gospel face-to-face with three lost Rock addicts. They understood the Gospel fine. Their hair, leather and studs didn't bother me, and my shirt and tie didn't bother them. It's the GOSPEL that does the relating, not Rock music or any other ungodly trick. The Holy Spirit's blessing is on God's Word, (John 17:17) not on pagan noise.

Do you know what those three headbangers told me during our meeting? They said, "Yeah, but it's O.K. for you CHRISTIANS to listen to 'Christian' Rock, isn't it?"

Something's dead wrong in the way we're "relating" to the lost, Brother and Sister. The WORLD is mocking and laughing at us! They see through such hypocrisy in a minute; why can't WE? It's because churches have made friends with their chains (2 Peter 2:19). They've been too busy listening to "the experts" instead of the

Holy Spirit (John 16:13 & 1 John 2:27).

3.) God created music, and everything God created is good, so Rock music must be good and godly, too.

Christian author LaMar Boschman's answer to this popular excuse is better than anything I could say. His reply is based on the scriptures found in Ezekiel 28:13 and Isaiah 14:11, which prove Lucifer's musicianship:

> "The day Lucifer fell, music fell. Music that once was used to worship Almighty God now became music of an earthly nature, it became the music of the world and began to appeal to our lower nature instead of appealing to God and our spiritual man (that part of us that has been born of God). Music then, became corrupted. That anointed and powerful ministry of music that Lucifer had in heaven is now corrupted. That ministry is cursed. It now has a false anointing... He still has that same powerful ministry to create worship but now it is corrupted, and Lucifer uses that ministry to get worship for himself because he craves it..."[1]

4.) Music is the universal language all young people understand, so we'll use Rock music to speak their language.

First of all, that's supposed to be impossible, because the doctrine of CCM says all music is neutral! But if it IS a language, then what is that music SAYING? This ad from CCM magazine is a perfect example of guilt-trip propaganda:

> "Ask any youth pastor or any parent of a teenager and they'll tell you the same thing: Most of today's praise and worship music simply does not reach today's teenagers. We all know that music is the language of teens, and let's face it: most of the praise and worship music available today is a foreign language to them. That's why youth leaders are having such a difficult time getting their kids involved in their worship services. Says one youth director, 'As hard as I try, my kids just sit back with their arms folded when we begin our praise times.' In order to communicate effectively, you must speak the right language..."[2]

Pastor and youth leader: if your young people are sitting on their hands during praise and worship time, the problem is in THEIR HEARTS, not the church's music! If you feed your kids the Rock and Rap slop they demand, they'll learn a new language alright - Satan's.

You know what? Once you start playing that game, they NEVER WILL BE satisfied, no matter what you do! "Give 'em what they want at any cost." Where's that found in the Bible? If you've got a youth group that's acting like poor, pampered little pouters, then demand their respect by refusing to cater to their rebellion.

In fairness to the kids, many youth won't give

up THEIR idolatry because the youth leaders won't give up THEIRS! (Jeremiah 5:31). Incidentally, the kids aren't supposed to run the church! God gave the man behind the pulpit that responsibility, and he is subject to Jesus Christ (Titus 1:7-2:1).

Churches in general demand very little (if anything) from their youth today. There's plenty of busywork - plays, skits, pizza parties, roller rinks, bowling alleys and water parks. But where's the hard, dedicated service? It's gone the way of the all-night prayer vigil, the family altar and godly teens. Dead and buried.

The results are obvious – weak, spiritually flabby Christian youth with no roots. This eventually leads to a stiff-necked generation who proudly parade spiritual arrogance, all the while mistaking it for holiness. It's the trap of the Pharisee mindset: "We've got it together. We know what we're doing and NOTHING is going to change our mind."

Praise God for the holy remnant. Not ALL churches are this way (Isaiah 1:9). If you feel alone in your stand against "Christian" Rock, be encouraged. The Lord Jesus is watching and your labor is not in vain (1 Corinthians 15:58).

5.) "No young person is going to stay in a 'stuffy' church. You've got to have some excitement! We've got to give the kids what they want or we'll lose them. Right?"

Wrong! If the only thing keeping the youth in your church is "Christian" Rock music, then let them go! If that's the glue holding the youth group together, you don't really have a youth group. To say that you must have Rock or the kids won't come is to dishonor and demean the drawing power of the Holy Ghost (John 6:44, 12:32). This ad for CCM star Morgan Cryar's music is a perfect case in point:

> "Fuel On The Fire - A good pop/rock sound for the teen-age audience. The songs deal with youth issues and situations without being preachy."[3]

Without being "preachy." To hear the CCM industry tell it, preaching the uncompromising Word of God is a fate worse than death. Someone might get turned off, and ruin their whole day. What does the Bible say?

> "For the **PREACHING** of the cross is to them that perish, foolishness; but unto us which are saved it is the power of God."
> 1 Corinthians 1:18

> "How then shall they call on him in whom they have not believed? and how shall they believe in him of whom they have not heard? and how shall they hear without a **PREACHER?**" Romans 10:14

> "I charge thee therefore before God, and the Lord Jesus Christ, who shall judge the quick and the dead at his appearing and his

> kingdom; *PREACH* the word; be instant in
> season, out of season; reprove, rebuke, exhort
> with all longsuffering and doctrine."
> 2 Timothy 4:1,2 (Emphasis author's).

If your church is dead, dry or "stuffy," then let some of the starch out! The Church should never be an organization; it's an organism – a living, vibrant body of believers.

If your church is full of snoring pew bums, don't think young people don't know it. They can spot a phoney a mile away. Give those kids something scriptural worth respecting, and they will. Keep feeding them gimmicks like "Christian" Rock, and you'll soon have contempt and rebellion coming out your ears (Proverbs 18:3).

SUBMISSION VS. REBELLION

The real battle is not about a musical generation gap, it's about SUBMISSION vs. REBELLION. Submission is the hallmark of the Christian life. Without it, all you have is counterfeit spirituality. To resist the devil, you must first be submitted to God (James 4:7). Since C-Rock fans aren't truly submitted, they'll never be able to resist Satan, no matter how often they sing "To Hell With The Devil" (by *Stryper*).

The classic hymns so despised by youth today were all about SUBMISSION; that's why carnal Christians want no part of them.

241

Songs like: "Washed In The Blood," "Haven of Rest," "Jesus Paid It All," "To God Be The Glory," "Lord, I'm Coming Home," "Victory In Jesus," "Have Thine Own Way, Lord," "When I Survey The Wondrous Cross," "Take My Life And Let It Be," "I Surrender All," "Jesus Is All The World To Me." These are all songs of SUBMISSION. Here's a lyrical example from just one of them:

"Have thine own way, Lord/ Have thine own way/ Thou art the potter/ I am the clay/ Mold me and make me/ After thy will/ While I am waiting/ Yielded and still..."

Now read these C-Rock lyrics to see the difference between submission and rebellion:

ROCK THOSE BLUES AWAY - Bride

"I don't need nobody to ease my aching mind. Don't need nobody complaining all the time. I need to roll those blues, rock those blues away... Let me tell you honey, what I need. I need a smooth playing guitar in my hand. Listen to the rhythm of my band."

Lots of godly submission in that one, isn't there?

If none of this describes your church, then shout hallelujah to the Lord, and back your pastor 100%, because he's standing strong against deception!

The 1990's will see the most intense war for the

souls of youth ever fought, and it's getting hotter by the day. The carnal, C-Rock supporting Church has already cut deals with the antichrist system (whether they know it or not). And they will cut many more in the weeks and months to come. Is YOUR church one of them?

6.) No one can live under those kind of rules! That's too hard and legalistic!

This is the most popular excuse in all of CCM. Submission to God cramps people's style. Someone might actually have to give up their desires and change their lives to make them conform to God's will. How harsh of God to ask us to obey Him.

Fortunately, Jesus was willing to obey the Father and give up the glory of Heaven to come to a filthy earth and die for our sins. Because of Christ's obedience, we can have eternal life. Where would we be now if Jesus Christ had used excuse # 6? (We'd be in hell.)

2 Timothy 4:3 predicted a time when Christians will not endure sound doctrine (That time is here right now). Isaiah 30:8-14 says many of God's people only want to hear "smooth things." The CCM stars are fulfilling these scriptures! They're trading sound doctrine for slick, carnal compromise by telling masses of believers that:

A. Music is neutral.

B. Jesus was a "cool dude" who would never want you to have a boring day, and

C. It'll all work out in the end, as long as you "feel good" about what you're doing.

This is rank apostasy of the worst sort, but plenty of duped Christians are eating it up like candy. Why? Because it's just what they want to hear.

Legalism is defined like this: LAWS WITHOUT LOVE. Pursuing Biblical holiness isn't legalism; it's real freedom! Knowing the truth sets people free, according to John 8:31,32.

Here's the truth, if you'll receive it: C-Rock music and everything it represents is satanic because it blocks the path to self-denial, purity, holiness and total devotion to the Lord Jesus.

There's only one foundation, and that's Jesus Christ (1 Corinthians 3:10-15). What we build on it is up to us. When that foundation gets cracked, weedy and full of garbage, it's time to clear aside the spiritual stumbling blocks and haul off the trash (Jeremiah 1:4-10). That's not legalism. It's repentance in action.

7.) I can't serve a God out of fear. Jesus is about love, and this music shows kids that.

There's nothing wrong with a good holy fear of

244

God. Those who truly love God WILL fear Him. The awesome, knee-shaking fear of God is a theme conspicuously absent from C-Rock music. (See Daniel 10:7-10, Isaiah 6:1-5, Ezekiel 1:28, 3:23, Hebrews 12:18-21, & Revelation 1:12-17). The C-Rock crowd is a perfect picture of what happens to people when there is no fear of God before their eyes.

Psalm 40:3 says our conversion will put a NEW song in our mouth that will cause those who hear it to FEAR! (Does C-Rock do that? They're too busy dancing!)

The fear of the Lord is the beginning of wisdom, (Psalm 111:10). Only by fearing God can we know what true godly love is. The fear of God is as Biblical as John 3:16.

8.) There's more important things in the church to worry about than music.

Satan would love for you to believe that lie. If "Christian" Rock is in your church, you've already got deception, rebellion and soul pollution in the minds of your young people. Anything more important than that?

If church leadership will diligently look, they'll see that MUSIC is a prime key to the spiritual health (or sickness) of any church. Preaching, teaching and the Great Commission are all major elements of the Body of Christ. And so is music. Don't ever sell it short.

9.) **Times have changed. It's time we changed too. The old ways don't work any more. We've got to update our approach and try something new. "Christian" Rock is the tool to better ministry.**

Those "old ways" you are tossing onto the garbage heap just so happen to be God's ways. They've worked for thousands of years, and no matter what any C-Rock fan tells you, they still work today.

When holy servants of God pray and clearly preach the Gospel, the Holy Spirit still convicts hearts and draws lost sinners unto repentance. Souls are still being saved every day. Here's how God sees it:

> "Thus saith the Lord, Stand ye in the ways, and see, and ask for the old paths, where is the good way, and walk therein, and ye shall find rest for your souls."
>
> Jeremiah 6:16

Do you dare to claim you've got a better plan for soulwinning than outlined in the Bible? If you do, I'd like to hear it, because that means you're smarter than God.

10.) As long as kids are getting saved, nothing else matters. So butt out, buddy.

When you reach this point in any discussion about CCM and all its ungodliness, it's time to stop, shake off the dust and move on. Any believer so bound will never understand the difference between the flesh and the spirit until God Himself makes it real to them.

They don't understand that fleshly lusts war against the soul (1 Peter 2:11). They won't accept the fact that flesh and spirit cannot peacefully co-exist (Galatians 5:16,17).

These are the people who go to dark "Christian" nightclubs and boogey all over the "Christian" dancefloor, while listening to "Christian" Rock. After all, the torture Jesus endured on the cross doesn't mean we can't have any fun. Right? God's heart breaks over such foolishness:

> "But I fear, lest by any means, as the serpent beguiled Eve through his subtilty, so your minds should be corrupted from the simplicity that is in Christ. For if he that cometh preacheth another Jesus, whom we have not preached, or if ye receive another spirit, which ye have not received, or another gospel, which ye have not accepted, ye might well bear with him." 2 Corinthians 11:3,4

The Church of Jesus Christ has ignored the obvious

for far too long. Excuses can be made from now until Judgment Day, but none of them will change one simple fact: there's nothing Christian about "Christian" Rock. You can make a list of excuses a mile long, but that's all they are – excuses.

My prayer is that you will see that God wants you to crucify your old flesh (Galatians 2:20) so Christ can live His life through you. I pray Jesus will change your affections form the inside out. Then you can learn to walk with God in ways you never thought possible.

It's the only way out of bondage, and I pray you'll take it.

FEEL FREE TO MAKE COPIES

If leadership in your church is pro-"Christian" Rock, feel free to photocopy this chapter as well as chapter 17 as a scriptural witness to them.

17

What God Says About Christian Rock

(*The Bible Speaks*)

Devoted fans of "Christian" Rock music feel secure in the knowledge that there is no scripture saying, "THOU SHALT NOT LISTEN TO 'CHRISTIAN' ROCK." They constantly sidestep clear Biblical teaching in dozens of different areas which blow C-Rock right out of the water.

The name of this game is , "Let Me Keep Sinning." But, praise God, the sharp two-edged sword of the Bible won't let anyone get away with it.

If you need scriptural proof that Rock music has nothing to do with Jesus Christ, the following verses are here for your study:

• **1 JOHN 3:4** "All unrighteousness is sin."
Is it a sin to listen to Rock music? This scripture says anything that's not right is sin. Rock music is either right or wrong; it can't be both. "Christian" Rock is either right or wrong; it can't be both. Since all Rock music (no matter what it's called) is based on rebellion, it will _never_ be right, because rebellion is as the sin of witchcraft, according to God's Word (1 Samuel 15:23).

• **EZEKIEL 22:26 and LEVITICUS 10:10**
There's supposed to be a DIFFERENCE between the holy and the profane. There's supposed to be a DIFFERENCE between the clean and the unclean. "Christian" Rock tries to erase that line. But facts can't be changed. Rock music is still profane, no matter what label anyone puts on it.

• **1 JOHN 2:15,16**
C-Rock not only LOOKS like the world, it IS the world! When your favorite C-Rock stars come out on stage wearing skin-tight spandex, hair teased to the moon, bombs blowing, smoke rolling and lights strobing, they are the lust of the eyes, the lust of the flesh and pride of life personified. Anyone who doesn't understand this is still in deep bondage to the flesh. Even the world has better spiritual discernment, and they're mocking us for our hypocrisy!

• **JAMES 4:4**
This verse says that to be a friend of the world is

to be the enemy of God. Rock music has the same effect on ALL people, regardless of the lyrics. C-Rock copies the world in every respect. When an ungodly sinner hears Rock music, he shakes, rattles and rolls. When a Christian CCM fan hears C-Rock music, he shakes, rattles and rolls. So what's the difference? To make friends with the world is to declare yourself God's ENEMY.

• **NUMBERS 21:3-6**
These verses apply perfectly to C-Rock today. God's people LOATHED godly provision. The things of God weren't GOOD enough for them. They wanted the things they had back when they were in bondage.

Isn't that the situation now? Old-fashioned, traditional Christian music isn't good enough anymore. Believers long for the same old worthless junk they had back in the days of bondage. They cry, "The old stuff doesn't feed me."

Speaking of being fed, 1 Corinthians 10:18-21 makes it clear that if you eat the sacrifice, you're a PARTAKER of the altar. Isn't "Christian" Rock music supposed to be a praise offering to the Lord? If you support C-Rock, you are PART of it. If it's a cup of devils (and it is), then you've just drunk a toast to Satan in the name of Jesus.

• **ROMANS 8:29**
God's desire for us is that we become like Jesus

Christ, conformed to His image. C-Rock paints a picture of a skin-head Jesus wallowing in the mosh pits, punching out innocent bystanders. That's not the Lord I serve. Jesus was pure and holy. He never partook in Satan's filth to accomplish God's perfect will.

• **2 CORINTHIANS 6:17**
> "Wherefore come out from among them, and be ye separate, saith the Lord, and touch not the unclean thing; and I will receive you."

It can't be said much plainer than that, CCM/C-Rock fan. Come out, be separate and don't touch unclean things. Since every other kind of muck funnels into it, *nothing* is filthier than Rock music.

• **ROMANS 12:2**
This one verse makes three important points every C-Rock fan needs to hear:

1.) "And be not conformed to this world."

Those who worship at the C-Rock altar pride themselves in their conformity to the world. Their goal and desire is to be as much like the world as possible. In fact, they're so much like the world, they don't even know what the world IS.

2.) "But be ye transformed"... (changed)

Your life is supposed to change when you get

saved. Christianity isn't supposed to change itself to suit you. It's the other way around. If there's been no change, you're not saved. It's that simple.

3.) "By the renewing of your mind."

Once saved, your mind should do a complete turnaround. You should be able to see this vile trash for what it really is. If you can't, then please read the final chapter of this book right now.

• GALATIANS 2:20

Through this verse and many others like it, God tells us to crucify the flesh. The whole purpose of C-Rock is to feed the rotten old flesh spirit until it gets good and fat. If you do the exact opposite of what God wants you to do, you're not pleasing God. And if you're not pleasing God, you're out of His Will, and subject to His rod of correction (Hebrews 12:5-14).

• EXODUS 20:3

The Bible says we are to worship *only* God, and have no other gods in our lives. CCM fans will argue, "I don't really WORSHIP it." How much time, energy and money do you spend on CCM tapes, CDs, posters and concerts? Is your room plastered with the trappings of C-Rock idolatry? Do you get mad when someone questions your favorite CCM star?

There's a word for this, it's "worship." And

worshiping anything other than God is called "idolatry." Idolators will NOT inherit the Kingdom of God (1 Corinthians 6:9).

• 1 CORINTHIANS 6:19,20

Maybe you're a C-Rock musician who feels "called by God." God never called anyone to destroy their body or their hearing to spread the Gospel. If you're truly saved, your body is the temple of the Holy Ghost. There's no way to justify destroying it by listening to (or playing) thundering C-Rock. Here's what prolonged exposure to Rock music ("Christian" or otherwise) will do to you:

> "In fact, the victim of hearing damage is passive - loud music can cause irreversible damage before a musician, or a member of a concert audience, is even aware that he or she is in danger of anything but a good time. Tinnitus itself is an annoying and unceasing ringing, rumbling, or staticky sound in the ears that rarely goes away. It can increase in its intensity to a level that has been horrifyingly described as being akin to 'holding a vacuum cleaner to your ear...'"[1]

If God truly called you into a ministry, there'll be a blessing in it. Where's the blessing in going deaf by 40?

• 1 JOHN 3:6,8

According to this scripture, if you continue willingly in sin, you are actually doing the work of Satan, not God. These verses show clearly that the average "Christian" Rock fan had best decide whether Rock music is right by GOD's standards, and forget what society says! It's YOUR spiritual future that's at stake. Who are you going to believe - the Bible, or some deluded musician who makes his money off your idolatry?

- **JEREMIAH 7:24-26**
    "But they hearkened not, nor inclined their ear, but walked in the counsels and in the imagination of their evil heart, and went backward, and not forward... I have even sent unto you all my servants the prophets, daily rising up early and sending them: Yet they hearkened not unto me, nor inclined their ear, but hardened their neck: they did worse than their fathers."

I'm giving it to you straight, C-Rock fans, because you deserve to hear the truth. Most of you haven't been alive long enough to have the slightest idea where Rock music came from, or why. Most of you could care less, anyway, because Rock & Roll is all you've ever known.

Match this scripture from Jeremiah against Rock history during the past thirty years. You'll find that it was bad for your parents to fill their minds with the ungodly screams of Rock music, but YOUR generation has done even worse! You've brought it into the house of God - the Church - and you've stiffened your neck as well.

255

If this makes you angry, then know for certain that even now you are under the conviction of the Holy Ghost. What you do or don't do about that conviction is up to you.

• 1 PETER 4:3,4
Once you're saved, old friends think it strange that you no longer run with them to the same useless, worldly junk. Unless, of course, you're a fan of "Christian" Rock. Then you've still got something in common with them – sin.

• HOSEA 7:8-10
These verses show the danger of MIXTURE. Did the Israelites win the pagan people of Canaan to the Lord when they mixed with their ways? No! Just the opposite happened. The Israelites WENT DOWN into the gutter. They still worshiped God, but the Lord became just one of many gods. Nothing has changed today. C-Rock fans worship the Lord; and all their Rock gods as well.

• JOB 14:4
This is a common sense scripture. It's IMPOSSIBLE to make something clean that is unclean. C-Rock defenders claim that filthy Rock music is now clean because it was claimed for the Lord. These scriptures say otherwise. Who's right, "the experts" or the Bible? (See Romans 3:4).

• NUMBERS 11:4-6
The Israelites' measured their happiness by what

they had while in BONDAGE. There's another name for this – it's called envy of the wicked. The same thing goes double in C-Rock/CCM today. Since church is supposed to be so BORING, Christians want what the world's got (and will come up with any excuse to keep it).

• HAGGAI 1:9-14
This scripture marks out the right path for God's people. When the remnant FEARED, things turned around real quick. When the people OBEYED and FEARED, the Lord moved. The Lord worked through them only after they OBEYED.

The entire CCM movement is founded on Rock music, the greatest symbol of rebellion ever unleashed on the modern world. Rebellion is the exact opposite of obedience, yet the C-Rock stars insist they ARE being obedient to God! What a satanic twist. Until these people regain the fear of God, they'll never understand the depth of their disobedience to Him (Psalm 111:10).

• JOB 36:8-13
"And if they be bound in fetters, and be holden in cords of affliction; Then he sheweth them their work, and their transgressions that they have exceeded. He openeth also their ear to discipline, and commandeth that they return from iniquity. If they obey and serve him, they shall spend their days in prosperity, and their years in pleasures. But if they obey not, they shall perish by the

> sword, and they shall die without knowledge.
> But the hypocrites in heart heap up wrath:
> they cry not when he bindeth them."

If you follow CCM, you have been shown your iniquity through the scriptures in this book. Now God commands you to stop your sin. God promises blessings if you will; and curses if you won't. Which will it be for you?

There are countless other verses that cut CCM to the bone. The Bible has so much to say about everything associated with the "Christian" Rock controversy, it would take an entire book to list them all. If you'll turn off the music and study the Bible instead, God will show you that 99.9% of CCM has nothing to do with Him at all.

Here's the end of the matter, straight from the Word of God.

• "Christian" Rock fans should: JAMES 1:22

• But instead, they: 2 PETER 2:18-22

• The end result being: HEBREWS 10:26,27

• The answer to the problem? 1 JOHN 1:8-10

18

Dave's Story - Testimony of an Ex-Christian Rocker

One hot July afternoon, I received a phone call from a young man in Kentucky named Dave.

My wife and I often get calls from all over the country, and we praise God for each and every one of them. This is one of the most exciting parts of this ministry because we never know what kind of person will be on the other end of the line.

We have had calls from angry "Christian" Rockers, confused, suicidal young people, godly pastors with a burden, slick manipulators out to make a name and a buck, and many a precious, praying saint who just wanted to encourage us in the work. Dave was from the first category. He was one mad C-Rock musician when I answered the phone:

> "You know that stuff you said about *Stryper*? Well, you were wrong, man. They really are saved and doing God's work. I've got hair down to my belt, and I play in a "Christian" Rock band. I suppose you're going to tell me I'm going to hell, right?"

I've learned from long, hard experience that the godly response to a hot accusation should NEVER be argument (2 Timothy 2:24-26). After quickly praying for wisdom, I layed out some scriptures for Dave's consideration. The conversation went something like this:

> "No, Dave, long hair doesn't send anybody to hell. The Bible says the only way people end up in hell is by NEGLECTING or REJECTING the blood of Jesus Christ. The only question that really matters is, where do you stand with Jesus? Has there ever been a time in your life when you asked Christ to save you from your sins, and meant it?"

Dave assured me that he had.

> "Alright. So Jesus Christ is your personal Saviour; is that right?"

The answer came back without any hesitation. "Yes."

"Good. 2 Corinthians 5:17 says that if any man be in Christ, he is a NEW creature. Old things are passed away; behold, ALL things are become new. That means after you accept Christ as your Saviour, there's supposed to be a complete CHANGE in everything about you. You're supposed to walk different, talk different, think different and even SMELL different. If that hasn't happened, something's wrong."

Dave considered this for a minute, then said:

"Before I got saved, I played in a Rock band and got involved in lots of sin. I don't do that stuff any more. I play for Jesus now, so everything's different. I mean, like I even play Dungeons & Dragons with my friends, and they're Christians. It's not like the occult, or anything, because we worship JESUS as we're playing. So that's not wrong, is it? I mean, I like songs like "Seventeen" by *Winger*. Just because that's not a Christian song, it's got a good message; there's nothing wrong with it."

I asked Dave what that Winger song was about and he replied:

"It's about an older man who really likes a younger girl a lot. But there's nothing bad about it..."

I decided to lay it right on the line:

"Come on. You're not THAT naive! That song's about a thirty-year old man having SEX with an

261

underage girl backstage. If you're really a Christian – and you just told me Jesus was your Saviour – then what's Jesus Christ going to say to you when He comes back and finds you playing occult garbage like D&D, or sitting in a room, jammin' out on the guitar, listening to trash like "Seventeen?" Jesus took the whip for you, Dave. The Bible says His visage was marred more than any man's. He was tortured and bled and crucified for YOU, and you're living like the devil. What's Christ going to say?"

There was a long pause as Dave thought. As I shared more scripture, his arguments grew less and less angry. God's Word was doing all the "relating" necessary. There was no need for me to out-smart, out-argue, use psychology, or pander to his "Christian" Rock addiction. The sharp, two-edged sword of scripture was doing the convicting.

We talked for another fifteen minutes. After hanging up, I prayed that God would take the seeds that had been sown and pierce Dave's heart with the truth about holiness and what it means to really be a Christian.

I was surprised to hear from Dave five days later, and was even more shocked at the change in his attitude. I was listening to a totally different person this time, and his testimony made my heart jump in my chest:

"Hey, this is Dave again. Remember me? I prayed

about what we talked about, and I've cut my
hair and burned all my records and tapes. Man,
I can't believe the difference in the way I feel.
My girlfriend's parents like me now, and
everything's so much better. I feel like I'm free."

"I even quit my 'Christian' Rock band. The other
band members really got mad when I told them
I was quitting. One of them took my guitar and
smashed it against the wall. I just looked at the
broken pieces and said, 'Thanks a lot. Now I
don't have to worry about getting rid of it.' "

Dave and I rejoiced together over the phone at
the miracle God had worked in his life. He ended
our conversation with a question:

"There's one thing I don't understand. I've asked
questions about the Bible to some of the heads
of the 'Christian' Rock movement in California,
and they couldn't give me any answers. Why is
that?"

I explained to Dave that the whole C-Rock
movement wants nothing to do with the Bible.
It's based on unscriptural philosophies and its
purpose is two-fold; making money and breeding
rebellion in young people.

I told him they don't really like what the Bible
says, despite the fact that real peace only comes
from reading and obeying God's Word – and
confessing and forsaking your sins, including sins
like C-Rock. I gave him a list of Bible verses to

study. He thanked me and hung up, happy and at peace. I sat stunned, and gave glory to God.

Dave called me two more times in the next few weeks. His next call was intense and serious:

> "Hey, this is Dave again, and I'm scared, man. I was out walking, and this van pulls up next to me with a guy driving, and these two girls in the front. He knew my name and the name of the band I used to play in. He told me those girls were fans of mine, and that for $50.00 I could have them both right there."

"What did you tell him?"

> "I said, 'No way man, I'm strong in Jesus, and I don't do that kind of stuff anymore'. Then this dude pulled a pentagram on a chain out from under his shirt and said, "I'm strong in SATAN! And we're gonna get you AND your girlfriend!' When he drove off, I saw two guys come up from the back of the van. Man, they wanted to get me. Somebody threatened to kill my grandmother on the phone. They knew her address and everything about her. I've got no idea who these people are, or why they're doing this. Man, I'm scared. What should I do?"

Dave and I prayed together for protection on him and his loved ones, and that Satan would be bound from off them, in the name of Jesus Christ. Then I shared a list of scriptures about God's power, and victory over the devil. I told Dave that Satan was furious over the fact that he had dumped "Christian" Rock. Now Satan was trying to scare him into coming back. The devil obviously had plans for Dave, and the Holy Ghost's conviction had blown Satan's scheme sky high. Greatly comforted by the Word of God and prayer, Dave said good-bye.

My last conversation with this former "Christian" Rocker came about two weeks later. He had good news:

> "I had a confrontation with those satanists, and God gave me the power to overcome them in the spirit. They weren't able to do anything to me, and they've left me alone now. I just wanted to call you again to tell you I've gotten married, and next week I'm checking out getting enrolled in a Bible college here. I want to be a music minister in a church, and really serve God the right way. I just wanted to say thank you, man, for being there. Because if it wasn't for our conversation, I don't know where I'd be today. Thanks, man. Good-bye."

I appreciated Dave's encouragement, but I knew the truth. If it wasn't for the power of GOD'S WORD combined with the Holy Ghost, his heart wouldn't have changed one bit. God taught me several good lessons from the whole experience, and I'd like to share them with you:

LESSON #1: "Christian Rock" breeds nothing but rebellion.

Dave's heart was hard; he was convinced he was right; and he could care less what anybody thought. HIS music couldn't be wrong, because everybody else caught up in the movement was telling him it was right. The ugly stamp of rebellion was all over him the first time we talked.

LESSON #2: The Word of God is all the "relating" anyone needs.

All Dave's years of "relating" through C-Rock did absolutely nothing for him spiritually. Yet two phone conversations where God's Word was presented and lifted up drove Dave to the Bible. Once he started reading the scriptures, God began work in Dave's life. It's no secret to real Christians that God blesses His Word, not the slam-banging noise at C-Rock concert halls.

C-Rock fans hate to hear it, but the common denominator that "relates" people through Rock music is called sin! No one who professes Jesus Christ as their personal Saviour should have anything to do with any Rock music, "Christian" or otherwise, because the angry, sensual, aggressive medium of all Rock music doesn't fit with a message of freedom from sin through Jesus.

If the hard, uncompromising power of the true Word of God was present in "Christian" Rock music, the concert halls would sit empty, and the musicians would dump their idolatry for REAL

266

scriptural music. So far, that's not happening. This tells me that the greatest excuse for C-Rock's existence is a total lie. The music doesn't bring the sinner to Christ – the BIBLE is the tool God ordained to get that job done (1 Corinthians 1:21, Romans 1:16).

LESSON #3: When real repentance hits, everything changes.

Once he realized his sin and repented of it, Dave's life did a complete turnaround. He could no longer live a lie and pretend he was serving Jesus, while living like the world. True, heartbroken repentance is what's missing in all C-Rock music. That's why masses of young believers are happy to keep serving Satan in the name of Jesus. The C-Rock stars have never repented of Rock idol worship, so why should the fans?

LESSON #4: When people repent, Satan gets mad!

One thing Satan can't stand is when people repent and turn their back on him and stop serving him. If you want to see Satan get mad at you, just repent and turn away from his C-Rock. You'll find out just how much he's deceived you with his religious music.

FINAL LESSON — There's more to "Christian" Rock than meets the eye.

Dave honestly thought he was serving Jesus Christ, yet when he repented and pulled out of the "Christian" Rock scene, it was the SATANISTS, not the Christians, who were mad at him.

Obviously, the satanists were using him all along, although he never knew it. They knew him, though he didn't know them. He was helping them, though he thought he was serving Christ. The bottom line is simple; rip away enough layers and you'll find the devil at the bottom of the C-Rock system.

Now what about YOU, "Christian" Rock fan? How do you KNOW the music you're involved in is really Christian? Because the gods and goddesses of C-Rock say so? How do you know the devil isn't even now pulling you into some sneaky trap by dangling his musical bait in front of your nose?

The only safe way to avoid Satan's schemes is to OBEY God's commands to be holy and separate from the world (James 4:4, 2 Corinthians 6:14-18). Anything less leaves the door wide open for Satan to play you for a fool.

Dave found out the truth, and got out before it was too late. What about you? Are you willing to play games with God, hoping He won't mind a little compromise? God doesn't play games, and neither does the devil.

You may think Dave's story is one in a million, but I get similar letters and phone calls all the time. From coast to coast, young people are finding out that "Christian" Rock music and the people that control it are playing a wicked con game of deceit and manipulation.

Satan's stamp is all over this music and those caught up in it. I pray you'll take Dave's testimony to heart and realize one simple fact:

If you support "Christian" Rock...

Satan has you right where he wants you!

19

What Do I Do Now?

ARE YOU IN C-ROCK BONDAGE?

You've read all the facts. Now it's time to make a decision. You have seen that the root of all C-Rock is based on rebellion. Its purpose is to harden your heart so you won't listen to someone like me when you are told the truth. But now you know the truth and it's decision time.

Before you decide what to do about your music, let's review some facts:

1. **CCM/C-Rock music brings no glory to Jesus Christ.**

2. **At best, the stars are money-grubbing compromisers.**

3. **The music's fruit is hard-hearted rebellion.**

4. It spits at all traditional Christian values, values put into place by God Himself in the Bible.

5. Its philosophies are not only un-biblical, they are totally against the Bible.

Why would you, as a Christian, want to have anything to do with that mess? And why would you fight to the death to defend it?

Why not face the facts? You have been led into grave deception by the enemy. Don't let that deception go on any longer. Break free from its grasp right now. Like Dave in chapter 18, you too can be rid of C-Rock obsession. Here's how:

If you're a Christian and you know it:

1. Pray that God will forgive you of the sin of idolatry, and every other sin associated with CCM worship.

2. Realize that fighting Satan's attacks requires an active, not a passive mind. You must submit yourself totally to God, then resist the devil. How? Bible reading, prayer, fasting, and confessing and forsaking your sins. If you will do these things, God promises the devil will flee from you. (See James 4:7)

3. Destroy every piece of Rock and "Christian"

Rock junk you own, (records, tapes, posters, magazines, etc.) just as the believers in Ephesus did in Acts 19:19.

If you're not 100% sure you're saved and on your way to Heaven, then please turn to chapter 20 right now.

If God has opened your eyes and you have destroyed all your C-Rock records and tapes, you may be asking, "So how am I supposed to fill that gaping hole that C-Rock used to fill? What am I supposed to listen to now?" Here are three alternatives to C-Rock and CCM you may consider:

1.) SILENCE

Did you know SILENCE is an alternative to ungodly music? Satan loves confusion, chaos, and noise. What the devil HATES is a home filled with the silent, blissful peace of God that passes understanding (Habakkuk 2:20, Psalm 46:10).

There's no law written anywhere that says you MUST listen to music. How many noisy years have you already wasted, blocked from hearing what God wanted to tell you, because you had a speaker in your ear?

Why not try some peace and quiet for a good, long time? You'll be amazed at how your mind and thoughts will clear out. It's a lot easier to hear God's voice when you are surrounded by silence than the sounds of ear-blasting noise.

2.) THE WORD OF GOD

One of the most overlooked alternatives to so-called Christian music is spending time reading the Word of God itself. This is how the Church hit the musical skids in the first place – by ignoring God's clear teaching! Few know (or even care) what the Bible demands from Christians. Who wants holiness when you can have every foul excess around, all in the name of Jesus?

When you throw the Rock and C-Rock garbage out of your tape player, why not put those decks to use with preaching tapes, or the Bible on cassette, and get REAL Scripture, instead of some CCM star's watered-down paraphrase? No true Christian needs an alternative to Jesus Christ.

3.) GODLY MUSIC

Godly music DOES exist! It's out there, but you'll really have to hunt for it. Music is not evil; it's a powerful and beautiful creation of Almighty God. Its purpose is not to fill up dead air space, but to bring us closer to our Lord and Saviour.

Many a sincere and confused Christian will rightly ask, "But how can I tell the difference? How can I KNOW what kind of music God really accepts?"

The first place to look is in God's Word. Start by getting a concordance, and looking up every reference to songs, singing, and music found in the Bible. If you want to know what kind of music God blesses, His Word will tell you.

Just one little verse in Colossians 3:16 has a wealth of wisdom for measuring music, if you break it up into sections.

- Godly music glorifies Jesus in both the words AND the music.

- Godly music has an anointing of either JOY or PEACE.

- A spirit of GRACE abides upon godly music.

- There is no PRIDE there.

- There IS much WISDOM.

- Godly music is RICH in teaching and warning, and comes straight from the heart. Godly music is never plastic, hyped-up, or contrived to fit some kind of Top 40 formula.

- Godly music consists of three types: Psalms, hymns and spiritual songs. SPIRITUAL songs – not hard-drivin', hip-shakin', brain-blasters.

You may be thinking, "Aw, can't you just give me a list of names, and I'll go out and buy 'em?" The whole purpose for this book is to get you to seek GOD's face instead of the "experts." There are no experts, except the Holy Spirit and God's Word. If you diligently seek God's face on your knees, with a broken heart and open mind, the Lord Jesus will lead you to the purest and most satisfying scriptural music you can imagine (Isaiah 66:2, Jeremiah 29:13).

IT'S UP TO YOU

Throughout this book, I have listed hundreds of Bible verses to prove what I've said. Now the work is up to the Holy Spirit. Please don't harden your heart any longer. Let the Holy Spirit speak to you. Then obey Him.

You'll find there's nothing sweeter than knowing you are standing in the direct center of God's Will because of obedience to His Word.

I'm praying right now for YOU as you read these words. It's my prayer that God will give you the knowledge, strength and wisdom to make the right choices at the right times. God can do it; He's just waiting for you to ask Him.

Why wait any longer? Ask Him right now.

275

20

What's Right About Jesus?

SALVATION

If you don't know without a shadow of a doubt what will happen to you after you die, I'm happy to share with you God's simple plan of salvation. Here is what the Bible says all must do to be saved from death, hell and eternal separation from God:

1. <u>ADMIT</u>
ADMIT you're a sinner. Romans 3:23 says ALL have sinned and come short of the glory of God.

2. <u>REPENT</u>
Be willing to REPENT (turn completely away)

from your sins. Jesus Christ said in Luke 13:5: "Except ye repent, ye shall all likewise perish". Romans 6:23 says:

> "The wages of sin is death, but the gift of God is eternal life through Jesus Christ our Lord."

3. BELIEVE AND CONFESS

You must BELIEVE deep down inside that Jesus Christ really is the Son of God who was sent to die for your sins and mine, and that He was raised from the dead. You must be willing to confess this publicly (Romans 10:9,10).

4. ASK

Finally, you must ASK Jesus Christ to forgive you of your sins, and come into your heart as your personal Saviour. Romans 10:13 says that whosoever shall call upon the name of the Lord SHALL be saved!

AFTER SALVATION

The Bible says anyone who means business with Jesus and cries out to Him for salvation will become a completely NEW creature (See 2 Corinthians 5:17).

If you really got saved and washed in the blood of Christ, here are some things that should be a natural part of you. If they are missing from your life, you need to get right with God – soon.

1. <u>READ THAT BIBLE</u>

If you're really saved, you'll be so hungry for the Word of God, you'll WANT to read it! No one should have to force you.

2. <u>TELL EVERYBODY</u>

If you're really saved, you won't be able to keep it to yourself. Whenever a chance comes your way, you'll tell others about what Christ has done in your life.

3. <u>PRAY, PRAY, PRAY</u>

If you're really saved, you'll have a deep need inside to talk to God every single day in prayer.

4. <u>OBEY GOD</u>

If you're really saved, the Holy Spirit will not let you get away with living a lie. Doing what God says to do in His Word will be a joy to you – not a boring chore. The more you learn to obey God, the greater blessings He will pour out on you. The opposite is also true.

HEALING

If you're already saved, but you've been playing games with God and the Lord Jesus, the Bible has a way out. 1 John 1:8,9 shows how:

> "If we say that we have no sin, we deceive ourselves, and the truth is not in us. If we confess our sins, he is faithful and just to

forgive us our sins, and to cleanse us from
all unrighteousness."

If you will get on your knees right now and confess
your sins to Jesus Christ, He just promised to
forgive them. Will you do it? Or will you try to
fight God? It's time to get serious about Jesus.

THE SHOW'S ALMOST OVER

The world system as we know it is falling apart
before our very eyes. Scripture after prophetic
scripture is being fulfilled world-wide. When
society finally crumbles, and the antichrist system
comes into full power, what will you do, and
where will you be?

When the Lord Jesus comes again, as He surely
will, you'll meet Him one of two ways: Either in
peace – or naked and ashamed:

IN PEACE

"Seeing then that all these things shall be
dissolved, what manner of persons ought
ye to be in all holy conversation and godliness,
Looking for and hasting unto the coming of
the day of God, wherein the heavens being
on fire shall be dissolved, and the elements
shall melt with fervent heat? Nevertheless
we, according to his promise, look for new
heavens and a new earth, wherein dwelleth
righteousness. Wherefore, beloved, seeing

279

that ye look for such things, be diligent that ye may be found of him in peace, without spot, and blameless." 2 Peter 3:11-14

NAKED & ASHAMED

"I counsel thee to buy of me gold tried in the fire, that thou mayest be rich; and white raiment, that thou mayest be clothed, and that the shame of thy nakedness do not appear; and anoint thine eyes with eyesalve, that thou mayest see. As many as I love, I rebuke and chasten: be zealous therefore, and repent." Revelation 3:18,19

Time is slipping away. I urge you in the name of the Lord Jesus Christ to sell out 100% and make Him the complete Lord of your life. Dump "Christian" Rock for good, and seek the real Jesus Christ of the Bible, not some cardboard cut-out.

The choice is yours: repentance and forgiveness or rebellion and shame forever. What's your decision? I pray you'll make the right one before it's too late.

POSTSCRIPT

For 13 years, I was a hopeless slave to Rock music. I played Heavy Metal for 7 years and worshiped Rock as my god. I spent thousands of dollars on everything associated with Rock & Roll and became a drug addict, alcoholic and criminal.

In September, 1984, I accepted the Lord Jesus Christ as my personal Saviour and He delivered me instantly from alcoholism, drugs and a criminal mind. There's been no turning back ever since. Glory to God for this great miracle.

All the knowledge gained while I was in bondage is now being used to expose Satan's dirty work in popular music, both through the books God has allowed me to write and through our five live Rock music seminars, which are being presented across the country and overseas.

I praise God for the opportunity to share the wonderful news that total freedom from all forms of Rock bondage is freely available through Christ.

Questions, comments and requests for information on scheduling live seminars should be sent to:

Jeff L. Godwin
The Rock Ministries
P.O. Box 2181
Bloomington, Indiana 47402

Footnotes

Chapter 1

1. Midnight Call, March, 1990, p. 6
2. Letter on file
3. KISS EXPOSED - Live Interview with the Peters Brothers, cassette tape, 1985, Truth About Rock, St. Paul, Minnesota.
4. CCM magazine, February, 1989, p. 21
5. Shame, a tract by Dr. Hal Webb, Conklin, New York, pp. 2,4,6

Chapter 3

1. Duluth News Tribune, October 9, 1987, p. 1C
2. The Closing Of The American Mind, by Allan Bloom, p. 73
3. The Toronto Star, February 10, 1990, p. K4
4. CCM magazine, November, 1988, p. 12
5. Christian Rock-A Strategem Of Mephistopheles, by Dr. David Noebel, P.O. Box 207, Manitou Springs, CO, 80829, pp. 12,25
6. Can God Use Rock Music?, by Keith Green, 1982, Last Days Ministries, Lindale, Texas
7. Ibid.
8. The Rolling Stones - An Illustrated Record, by Roy Carr, 1976, Harmony Books, New York, p. 37
9. Face The Music - Contemporary Church Music On Trial, by Leonard J. Seidel, 1988, Grace Unlimited Publications, 7124 Freshaire Dr., Springfield, Virginia, 22153, pp. 46-51
10. Jarring Music Takes Toll On Mice, by Richard Lipkin, Insight, April, 1988, p. 58
11. The Secret Power Of Music, by David Tame, 1984, Destiny Books, pp. 141-145
12. Can Rock & Roll Lead To Rack & Ruin, by Mark Grant, LA Times, February 5, 1978
13. Christian Rock - A Strategem Of Mephistopheles, p. 27
14. How To Recognize 'The Lie' In Contemporary Music, pp. 129-133
15. Ibid. pp. 129-133.
16. Ibid. pp. 129-133.
17. Frank Garlock, Bob Jones University, Greenville, South Carolina.
18. Ibid.
19. Letter on file
20. Letter on file

Chapter 4

1. The Satan-Seller, by Mike Warnke, with Dave Balsiger & Les Jones, 1972, Bridge Publishing. Inc., South Plainfield, N.J., pp. 88,100
2. The Life And Times Of Little Richard, by Charles White, 1984,

Pocket Books, New York, p. 197

3. Hellfire - The Jerry Lee Lewis Story, by Nick Tosches, 1982, Dell Publishing Co. Inc., New York, pp. 130,132,245
4. Media Update, May/June, 1987, pp. 3,4
5. World Book Encyclopedia, 1969, Volume 16, p. 481. Also see "The Satan Hunter," by Tom Wedge & Robert L. Powers, 1988, Daring Books, Canton, Ohio, p. 195
6. Long Haired Christian Soldiers, by Peter Wilmoth.
7. Sunday People, October 30, 1988
8. SPIN, December, 1989, p. 107
9. Holy Rock And Rollers!, by Michael Small, p. 70.
10. Treasury Of Witchcraft, by Harry E. Wedeck, 1961, Citadel Press, p. 111
11. RIP, June, 1989, p. 41
12. CCM magazine, August, 1990, p. 10
13. CCM magazine, March, 1990, p. 15
14. Robert Sweet's Story, Stryper fan club promotional material.
15. Michael Sweet's Story, Stryper fan club promotional material.
16. Christian Or Religious Rock-The Controversy Confronted, by Glen Berteau, 1986, Tape # 2
17. The Sun, April 4, 1989, p. 7
18. Ibid.

Chapter 5

1. Ravaged By The New Age, by Texe Marrs, 1989, Living Truth Publishers, Austin, Texas, p. 80
2. Media Update, September/October, 1989, p. 3
3. Spiritualists of Rock, by Paul Mansfield
4. Ibid.
5. The People, October 23, 1988, p. 15
6. Rock, by Bob Larson, 1984, Living Books, Wheaton, Illinois, p.140
7. The Hidden Dangers of The Rainbow, by Constance Cumbey, 1983, Huntington House, Inc., Shreveport, Louisiana, pp. 58, 65, 66; & World Book Encyclopedia, 1969, Vol. 12, p. 446
8. Ibid. pp. 177, 178
9. Photostat on file
10. The Trail of The Serpent, by Inquire Within, p. 253
11. Light-Bearers of Darkness, by Inquire Within, p. 73
12. Ibid. p. 74
13. Media Update, November/December, 1986, p. 19
14. CCM magazine, March, 1990, p. 52

Chapter 6

1. Gospel Music Today, April/May/June, 1987, p. 28

2. Ibid. p. 22
3. CCM magazine, January, 1989, p. 14
4. Media Update, September/October, 1989, p. 11
5. CCM magazine, April, 1987, p. 38
6. Media Update, September/October, 1989, p. 11
7. Gospel Music Today, July/August/September, 1987, p. 34
8. Gospel Music Today, July/August/September, 1989, p. 10
9. Christian Amy's No Rock 'n' Roll Sinner, by Bruce Guthrie.
10. Oz magazine, 1987, Queensland, Australia, p. 14
11. CCM magazine, January, 1989, p. 30
12. Echoes, Vol. 2, 1986, p. 7
13. CCM magazine, January, 1989, p. 31
14. CCM magazine, February, 1990, p. 22
15. CCM magazine, April, 1990, p. 52
16. Youth!, January, 1987, p. 8
17. Circus, November 30, 1984, pp. 52,53. Photo by Mark Weiss.
18. CCM magazine, February, 1990. p. 15. No photo credit listed.
19. Satanic & Hidden Messages in Popular and Rock and Roll Music, by Michael M., 1989, Melbourne, Australia, Tape 6, Example 275
20. CCM magazine, September, 1988, p. 47
21. Christian Rock? Christian Rap?, by James A. Thomas, 1989, Salinas, California, p. 9
22. Metal Mardi Gras 1987 video, by Sanctuary, Redondo Beach, CA, a C. Cole production
23. Good News Journal, Summer, 1989, Columbia, Missouri.

Chapter 8

1. CCM magazine, October, 1988, p. 13
2. Ibid.
3. Ibid.
4. Ibid.
5. Ibid.
6. Christian Amy's No Rock 'n' Roll Sinner, by Bruce Guthrie.
7. Family Circle, September 9, 1986, p. 24
8. Ibid.
9. CCM magazine, December, 1988, p. 38
10. CCM magazine, January, 1989, p. 20
11. Christian Activities Calendar, Spring/Summer, 1989, p. 11
12. CCM magazine, November, 1987, p. 8
13. CCM magazine, November, 1988, p. 8
14. Echoes, Vol. 2, 1986, p. 14
15. Christianity Today, October 2, 1987, p. 59
16. CCM magazine, October, 1988, p. 21
17. Rock Music - What's The Real Message?, interview by Pastor

Mark Anderson, Minneapolis, Minnesota, pgs. 2,3.
18. Ministries Today, January/February, 1987, p. 28
19. Rock Music - What's The Real Message? Part 2, interview by Pastor Mark Anderson, Minneapolis, Minnesota, p. 3.
20. Photostat on file.
21. Ministries Today, January/February, 1987, p. 30

Chapter 9
1. Last Trumpet Ministries newsletter, Vol. VII, Issue VI, June, 1988, P.O. Box 806, Beaver Dam, Wisconsin, 53916, p. 2
2 . Backwards Masking - How Subliminals Affect You, by the Peters Brothers, 1983, Truth About Rock, St. Paul, Minnesota, pp. 2,4,5,10-12,16,17
3. Rock's Hidden Persuader: The Truth About Backmasking, by Dan & Steve Peters, with Cher Merrill, 1985, Bethany House, Minneapolis, Minnesota, p. 13
4. Subliminal Tapes Big Business, Monroe, Louisiana News-Star, January 28, 1990
5. The Love Tapes catalog, 1988, Edina, Minnesota, p. 16
6. The Love Tapes catalog, 1988, Edina, Minnesota, p. 17
7. The Love Tapes catalog, 1988, Edina, Minnesota, p. 21
8. The Love Tapes catalog, 1988, Edina, Minnesota, p. 21
9. Charisma & Christian Life, February, 1990, p. 96
10. Media Sexploitation, by Wilson Bryan Key, 1976, Signet Books, New York, pp. 14,117
11. Life magazine, October 3, 1969, p. 74
12. Life magazine, October 3, 1969, p. 74
13. "Jamie's Got A Gun", by Deborah Cameron, Good Weekend magazine, June 9, 1990, p. 13
14. Ibid. p. 11
15. Satanic and Hidden Messages in Popular and Rock and Roll Music, by Michael M., 1989, Melbourne, Australia, Tape # 1
16. Ibid.
17. Letter on file.
18. Satanic and Hidden Messages in Popular and Rock and Roll Music, Tape # 2, Example # 62
19. Photostat on file.
20. Last Trumpet Ministries newsletter, Vol. IX, Issue 11, February, 1990, P.O. Box 806, Beaver Dam, Wisconsin, 53916, p. 3
21. Photostat on file.
22. Ravaged By The New Age, by Texe Marrs, 1989, Living Truth Publishers, Austin, Texas, p. 213
23. Battle Cry, Chick Publications, Cucamonga, California, September/October, 1987, p. 4

24. Letter on file.
25. Satanic and Hidden Messages in Popular and Rock and Roll Music, Tape # 5, Example # 190
26. Satanic and Hidden Messages in Popular and Rock and Roll Music, Tape # 5, Example # 179

Chapter 10

1. Who Do You Listen To? music video soundtrack, 1989, Word, Inc., Waco, Texas
2. CCM magazine, April, 1990, p. 38
3. Rap: Straight From the Streets cassette tape, 1990, the Benson Co., Inc., Nashville, Tennessee
4. Face The Music - Contemporary Church Music On Trial, by Leonard J. Seidel, Grace Unlimited Publications, 7124 Freshaire Dr., Springfield, Virginia, 22153, pgs. 36,37,38
5. CCM magazine, April, 1990, p. 41
6. Ibid.
7. Youth!, January, 1988, p. 13
8. How To Win Over Depression, by Tim LaHaye, p. 187
9. Youth!, January, 1988, p. 15
10. Charisma & Christian Life, February, 1990, p. 42
11. Youth!, January, 1988, p. 15
12. Youth!, January, 1988, p. 15

Chapter 11

1. Newspaper clipping photo on file. No photo source listed.
2. Faces Rocks, May, 1987, p. 23. No photo source listed.
3. Metal Edge, "Metal's Messiahs - Praise the Loud: Righteous Rockers Spread the Word", p. 51. No photo source listed.
4. Ibid.
5. Faces Rocks, May, 1987, p. 22. No photo source listed.
6. White Throne, No. 5, 1989, p. 22. No photo source listed.

Chapter 12

1. Lyrics to the song, "Video Action", by DeGarmo & Key
2. "Live... Radically Saved" video, 1988, the Benson Co., Inc., Nashville, Tennessee
3. Ibid.
4. Ibid.
5. Ibid.
6. Ibid.
7. Ibid.
8. CCM magazine, February, 1990, p. 13